la Biennale di Venezia

57. Esposizione Internazionale d'Arte

Partecipazioni Nazionali

Contents

Foreword

It is with great anticipation, joy, and confidence that we present the 2017 edition of the Nordic Pavilion at La Biennale di Venezia. At this 57th International Art Exhibition, the biennial of biennials, which has existed for more than one hundred years now, we can also note that the Nordic Pavilion has hosted Finland's, Norway's and Sweden's collective undertakings for nearly half a century. With a renewed agreement, entailing that the three nations commit to produce a joint project for the period 2017 to 2021, Nordic cooperation is once again reinforced. The principal responsibility for the exhibition will rotate between the countries, with Sweden next in turn.

Mirrored is a group exhibition featuring works by six artists from different generations: Siri Aurdal, Nina Canell, Charlotte Johannesson, Jumana Manna, Pasi "Sleeping" Myllymäki, and Mika Taanila. They all share an experimental approach, which for the older generation takes the form of module-based sculptures, translations of textile crafts into computer animations, or performative actions with the camera as their instrument. Material-based processes and social issues also preoccupy the younger generation, whose cinematic montage techniques, sculptural displacements of spatial perception, or explorations of power relationships will claim the pavilion's open architecture.

We wish to extend our warm thanks to the curator, Mats Stjernstedt, for his sensitivity to the space and the assignment's complexity when undertaking this challenge in an innovative and respectful spirit, and for his exemplary collaboration with Moderna Museet's curator, Matilda Olof-Ors, the project manager of the exhibition. We also thank the six artists profusely, for the time and enthusiasm they have devoted to the entire project and their invaluable contribution in the form of adaptations of previous works and entirely new productions.

Thanks, also, to the catalogue authors, Kirsty Bell, Edwin Carels, Tytti Rantanen, Chris Sharp, Cecilia Widenheim, and Kaelen Wilson-Goldie, who have delivered insightful keys to understanding these artists, and to Stefano Cernuschi with Marco Fasolini at Mousse Publishing in Milan, who devised the book's congenial design.

Finally, huge thanks to those who have loaned art to the exhibition, for generously enabling us to show important works for almost a year. A project of this caliber is largely financed by the organizers, that is, Frame Contemporary Art Finland, Moderna

Museet, and Office for Contemporary Art Norway (OCA), but it would not have been possible without additional support from others. Our heartfelt thanks to the Barbro Osher Pro Suecia Foundation for their very generous contribution, and equally warm thanks to the Nordic Circle for Venice, a new initiative for supporting the Nordic Pavilion.

Ann-Sofi Noring
Moderna Museet

Katya García-Antón
Office for Contemporary Art Norway (OCA)

Raija Koli
Frame Contemporary Art Finland

Introduction
Mats Stjernstedt

I am greatly pleased to have been granted this opportunity to invite Siri Aurdal, Nina Canell, Charlotte Johannesson, Jumana Manna, Pasi "Sleeping" Myllymäki, and Mika Taanila to participate in the exhibition *Mirrored*, to be shown at the Nordic Pavilion during the 57th International Art Exhibition, La Biennale di Venezia.

The artists in this group have taken distinctly unique approaches to exploring sculptural and pictorial transformative processes through the use of political and material content, moving images, and digital or architectural space.

In part, the subject matter of the exhibition *Mirrored* is the architecture of the site where it is shown: the Nordic Pavilion, which was built between 1958 and 1962. The structure presents an architectural scenery consisting of both surface and depth, in that the space is sealed behind glass windows. This allows the viewer to move around it, but also access it through a system of flexible entrances.

In line with Guiliana Bruno's discussion of how humans relate to their reflections, the mirror is suggested to constitute, as well as give rise to, a "placeless place," to use a phrase she borrows from Foucault. The use of the allegory of the mirror is intended to move the focus of the discussion away from the characterisation of art in accordance with national boundaries. Instead, the emphasis is on the participating artists, and how their practices illuminate the various ways in which boundaries can be, and are, dissolved and crossed.

The exhibition in the Nordic Pavilion is installed as a loop in which figuration, material, technology, and execution process gradually succeed one another. Jumana Manna's *Government Quarter Study*, which consists of three tripartite columns, form a visual corridor: an architecture serving as an entryway to architecture. More generally, Manna's work can be said to be an exploration of how power is articulated through relationships, often focusing on the body and materiality in relation to histories of place. In her sculptural work, Manna indirectly unfolds representation, creating a visual language of absence and substitutes.

Within the looped structure of the exhibition, material passes through stages of rigidity and elasticity, from supportive and enfolding properties to time-based process and material collapse. The juxtaposition of Siri Aurdal's and Nina Canell's sculptural works reveals a connection across time in their thoughts on how to portray aspects of communication through material and immaterial sculpture. In Aurdal's case, this is expressed through her preoccupation with sculpture as a synthesis of space and the architecture in which human beings exist and interact; in Canell's work, it resides with her use of the actual technology we use to communicate with one another in this digital age.

The innovator Charlotte Johannesson is an artist who developed her interest in creating pictures through weaving to incorporate the early digital imaging methods used in the first generation of personal computers. In the digital workshop they ran in the 80s, she and her partner Sture Johannesson invented the technology that would allow her to translate the imagery that was to become her own artistic realm.

Between 1979 and 1986, Pasi "Sleeping" Myllymäki was engaged in an intense exploration of the creative use of 16mm film. Myllymäki's films, apart from depicting the alternative underground that the Punk and New Wave cultures introduced to Finland, present a both witty and tireless experimenting with cameras, performance elements, sound, and DIY soundtracks, all of this carried out in dialogue with his partner in crime, Risto "the Legend" Laakonen.

For this exhibition, Mika Taanila, best known for

his film and sound installations, has produced a new series of works based on books and other literature on film. Applying methods and strategies familiar to him from his work as a director and editor of film to printed matter, Taanila manages to produce a new situation. Here, his aesthetic interventions in cutting up the material result in a kind of archaeology of film, while simultaneously producing both dramatic and violent consequences.

I would like to thank all the participating artists for their dedication and absolute commitment to this Nordic Pavilion exhibition, which they have expressed through their ideas and their efforts in working on their contributions.

I would also like to give warm thanks to the Nordic Committee: Ann-Sofi Noring of Moderna Museet, Raija Koli of Frame Contemporary Art Finland, and Katya García-Antón of Office for Contemporary Art Norway (OCA).

Special thanks go to the owner's group via Siri Berg, of Statsbygg in Oslo, for the dialogue we've shared throughout the planning and installation processes, and for their understanding of the artist's intentions.

Thanks are also due to Teresa Hahr and Guy Engström for their help and support in the work producing this exhibition catalogue.

In closing, I would like to extend my greatest and warmest thanks to my closest co-worker, project manager Matilda Olof-Ors.

Siri Aurdal

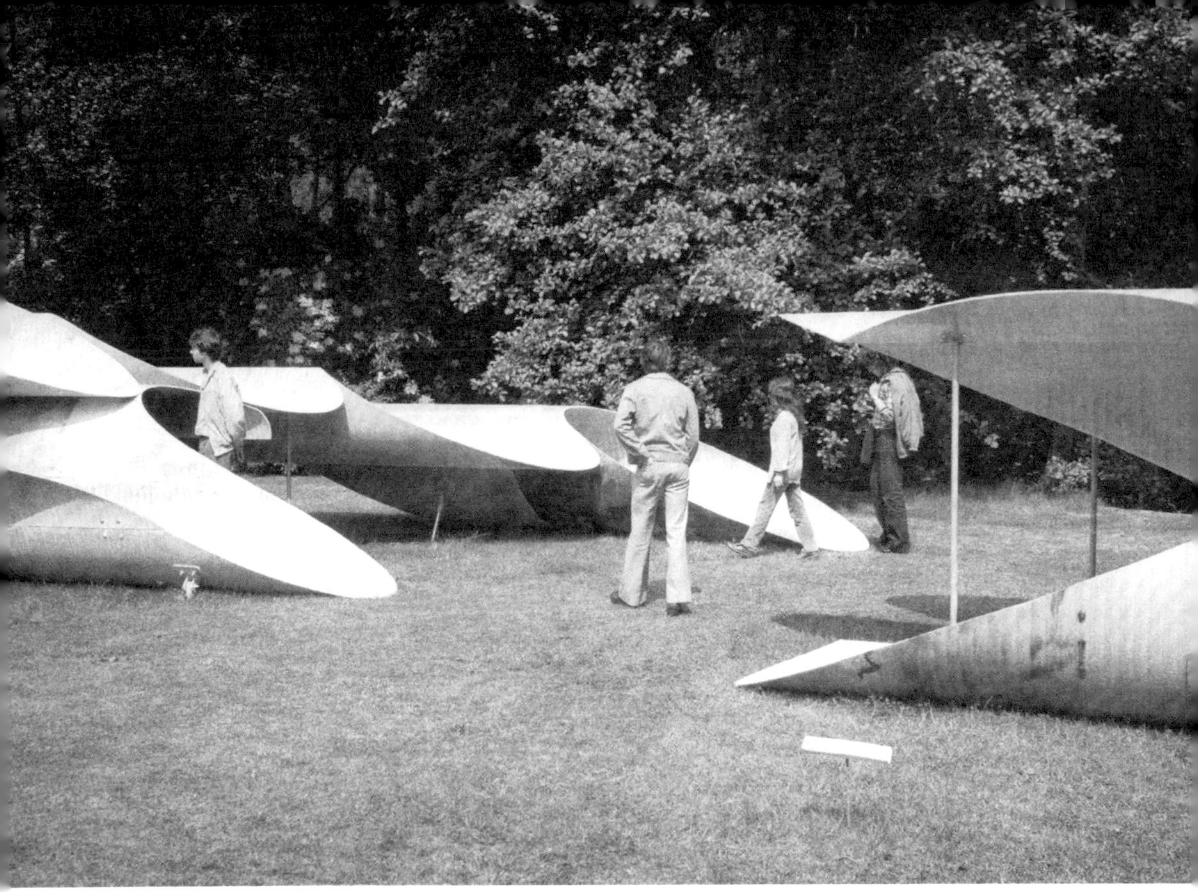

Greeting to the Lucas Workers
15th Sculpture Biennale in Middelheim,
Antwerp, 1979

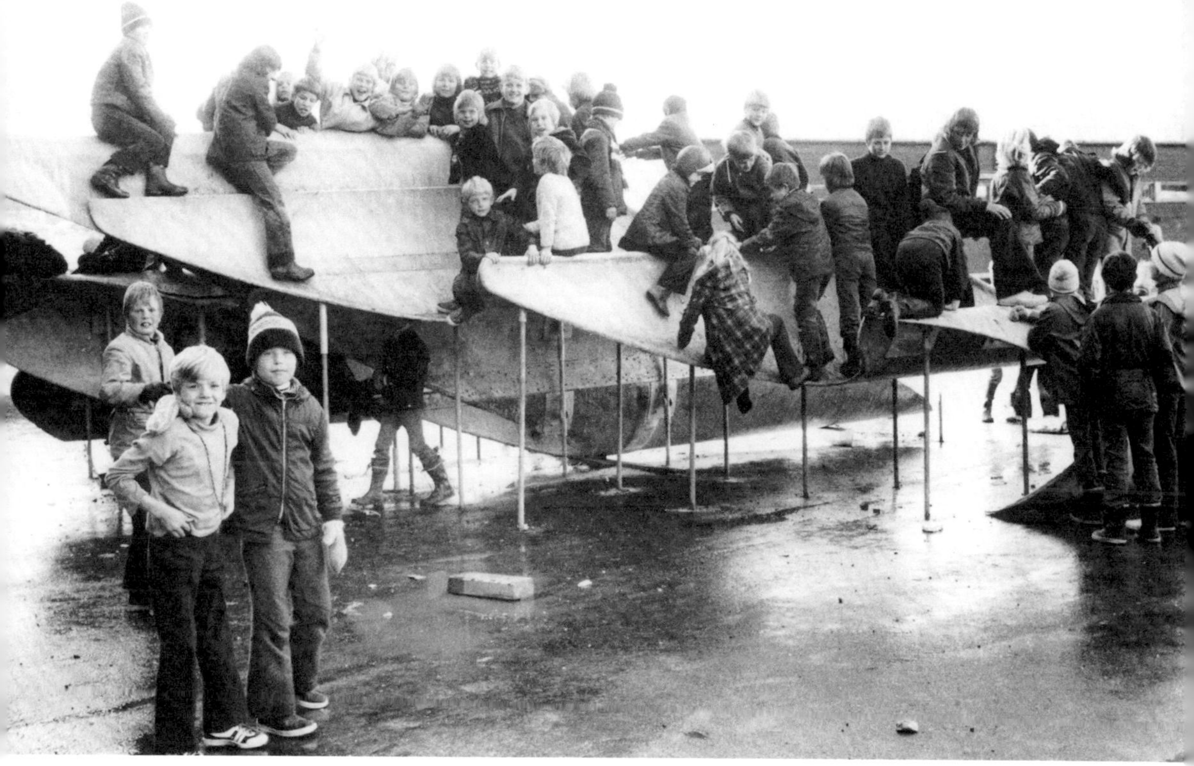

Havbølger, 1972
15 Trosterud Elementary School, Oslo

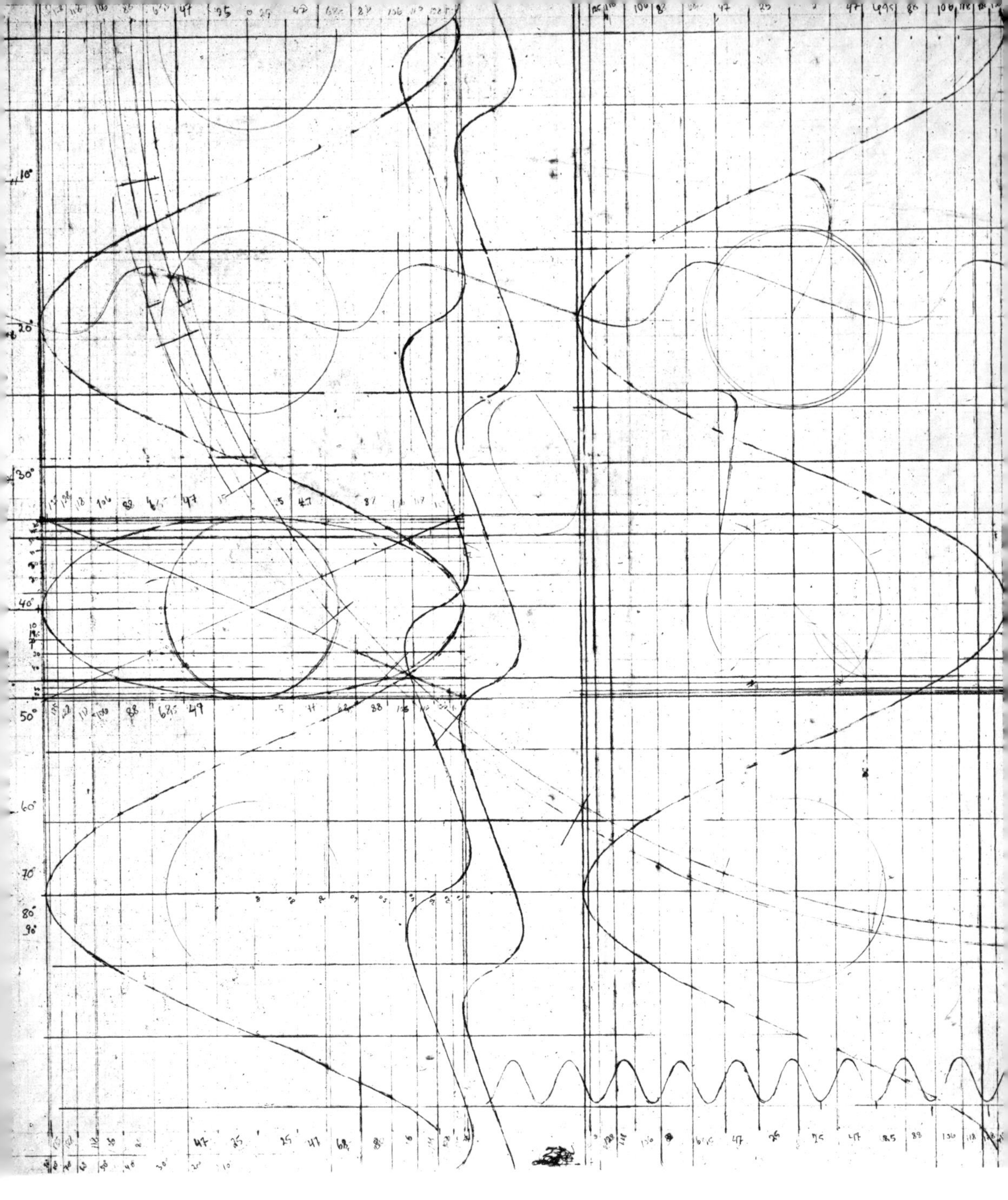

16 Technical drawing on acetate, 1960

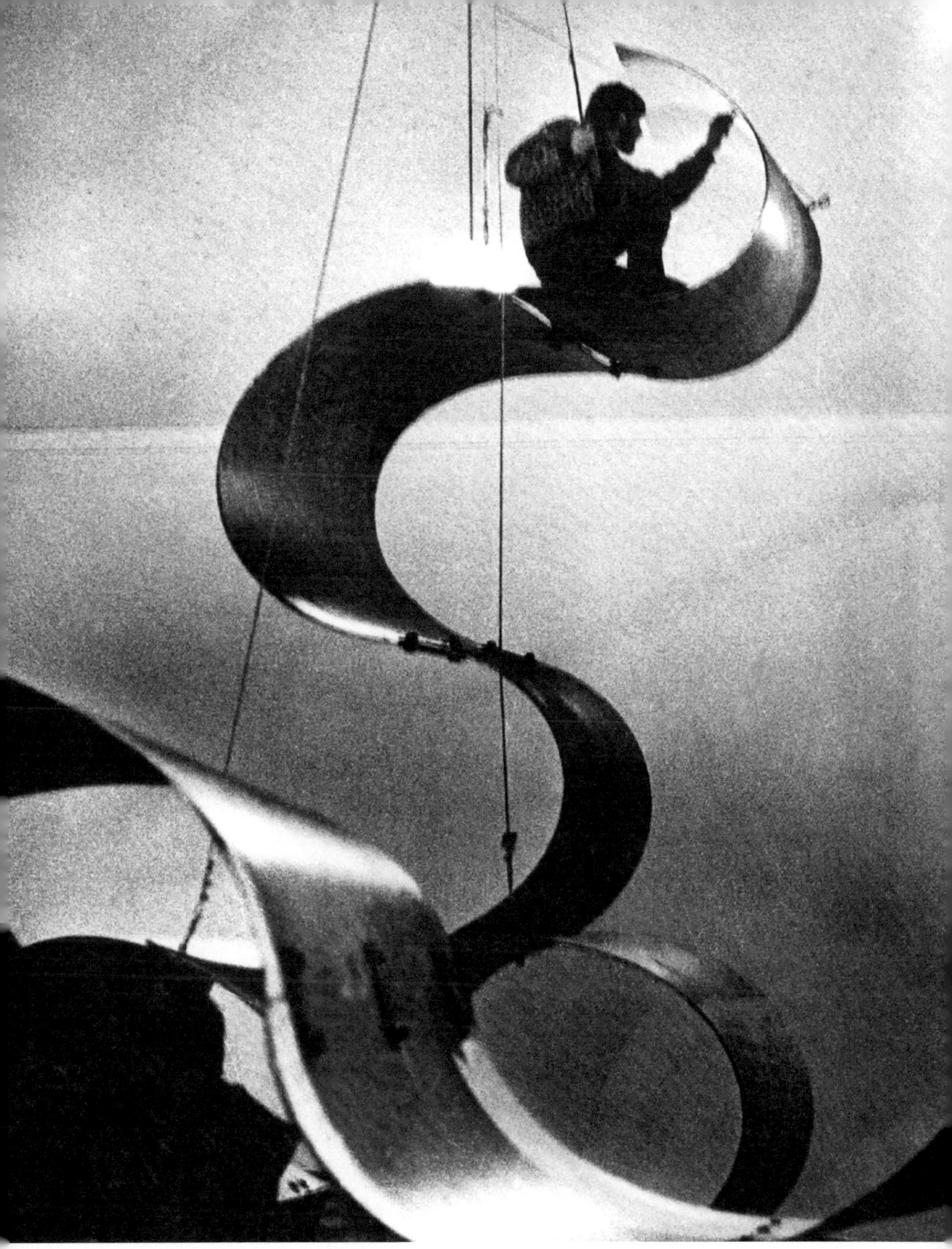

Surroundings
Installation with cut PVC pipelines
Installation view, Kunstnernes Hus, Oslo, 1969

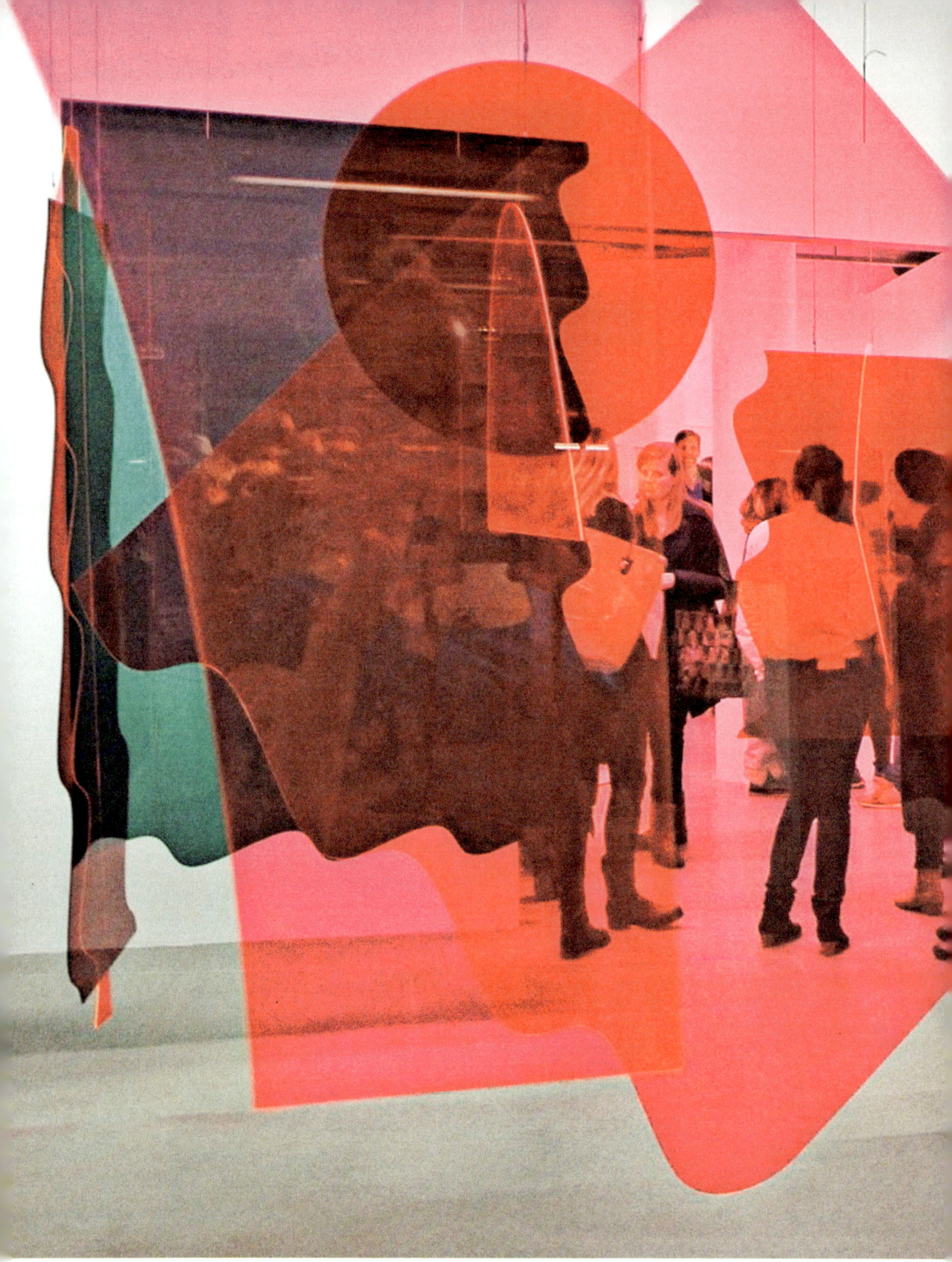

Interview, 1968–2013
Plexiglas, dimensions variable
Installation view, Kunsthall Oslo, 2013

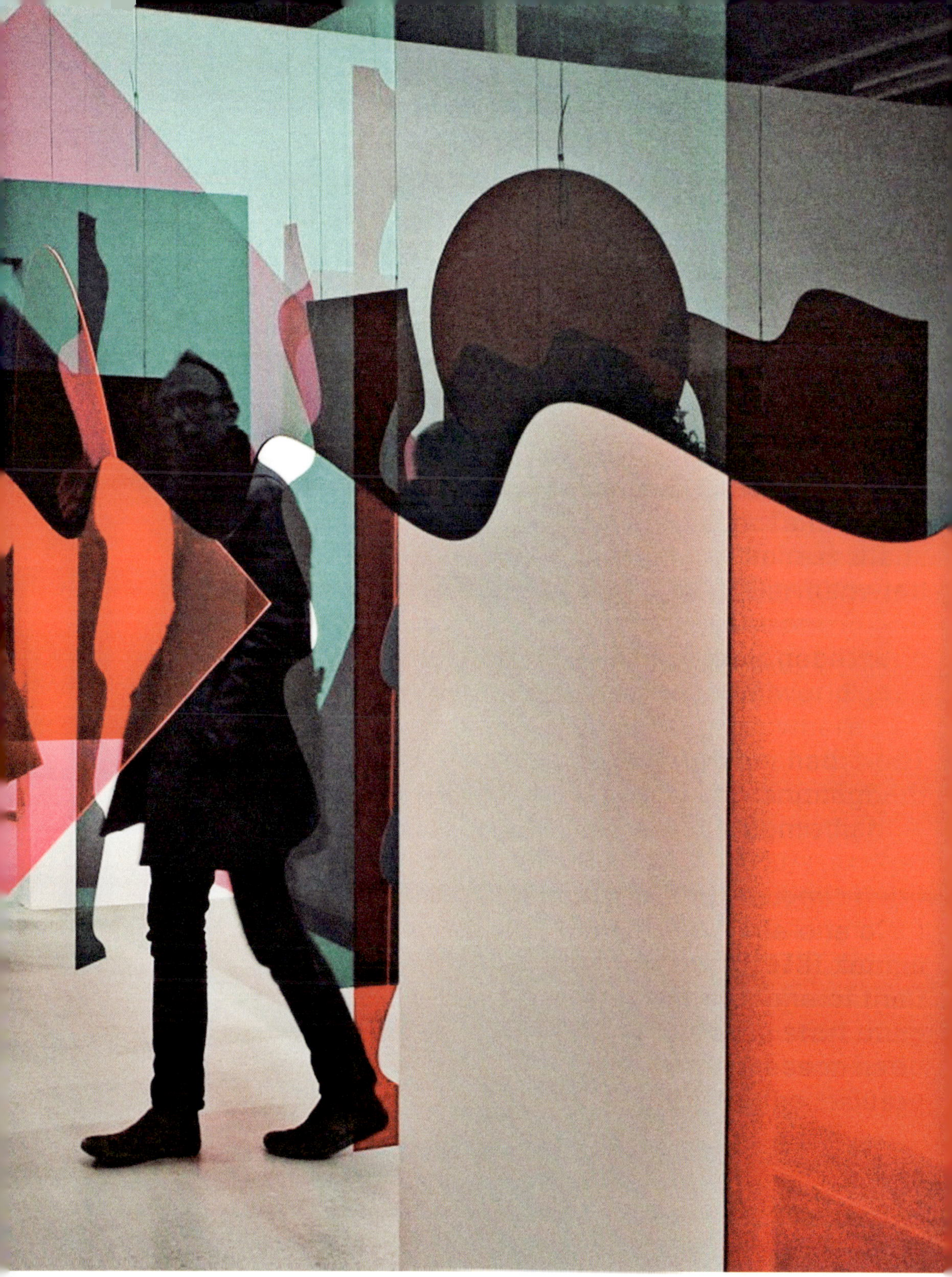

Siri Aurdal: Aspects of a Living Sculpture
by Kirsty Bell

A group of sculptures built of tubular fiberglass in pale pink and greenish-gray tones occupies the upstairs gallery of Oslo's Kunstnernes Hus. Their modular construction is clearly legible: sections of pipe, a meter or so in diameter, cut on the diagonal and joined together to make wavelike curves. More striking, however, is their effect on the visiting public, who sit or recline on the curving planes, or crawl through the interior spaces. Made by the Norwegian artist Siri Aurdal (b. 1937) and titled *Bølgelengder* (Wavelengths), the structures' sharp curves establish and describe a relation between inside and outside, form and space, that proposes an inhabitable interior, activating both the architecture of the room and the people who encounter it.

The presence of these sociable structures in the Kunstnernes Hus in 2016, shown together with photographs by Eline Mugaas, is a reprise. Aurdal's first iteration of the work, titled *Omgivelser* (Surroundings), was made for and shown in this same exhibition space almost fifty years ago, in 1969. At that time, the factory-ready nature of its materials—giant fiberglass-coated polyester pipes developed for the nascent oil industry—pointed presciently toward industry and its attendant economy. (Norway struck oil just months after the work went on show.) Around this time, Aurdal had become involved in a collaborative graphics workshop named GRAS, established to address the sociopolitical unrest that was in the air in the late 1960s. The director of Kunstnernes Hus, the artist Morten Krohg, was also an active member of GRAS, and together they invited fellow artists to paint and write on the sculptures. Pictures from the time have the unmistakable aura of late-1960s utopianism: groups of people congregate to talk under the structures' flowing, roof-like curves, while others scale to the summit to daub the work with painted slogans: "Kunstnerlønn til hele folket!" (Artist wages for all the people!). The political was inscribed, literally, onto the work's surface in a dense graffiti, and figuratively in its purpose as a place for congregation.

After its initial exhibition in 1969, this system of diagonally cut lengths of pipe became a kind of ur-system for the artist, continually reworked and constructed in different combinations. Even in 2016, once the show at Kunstnernes Hus closed, Aurdal's work was moved to Oslo's Vigelandsparken, a transition the artist described as a "recomposition," renaming it *Bølgelengder rekomponert* (Wavelengths Recomposed). Occupying a patch of grassy parkland, it now became a resting place or climbing frame for the park's visitors.

Aurdal had always conceived of it as a continually modifiable entity—more system than sculpture, both provisional shelter and open-ended proposition—designed to construct fluid forms without beginning or end.

* * *

Aurdal was born in 1937 into a family of artists—both her mother, Synnøve Anker Aurdal, and grandmother, Gudrun Anker, were renowned for their work with textiles—but she wanted to study architecture. When she wasn't accepted by the architecture school, still very much a male territory in 1958, she signed up for sculpture at Oslo's Art Academy, followed by a scholarship to Paris in 1961–62. Her earliest work was figurative—busts and portraits roughly hewn in concrete or cast in bronze—but the prolific drawings she made throughout the 1960s show her interest in figure and face increasingly turning to contour, extrapolating forms into dynamically fluid lines, a soft geometry, while suggesting the space around an object or figure to be just as important as the object or figure itself. By the mid-1960s she was sketching and building models for more architectural structures, such as columns or fountains, composed of modular geometrical forms.

One of Aurdal's first spatially oriented works was *Mobile*, made for Oslo's Galleri Kringla, an artist-run space, in 1968. Large sheets of colored Plexiglas cut into wave patterns were suspended from the ceiling to create a series of room-like spaces through which visitors could move and socialize. This work signaled a return to her interest in architecture, and was inspired by two experiences of social environments from her time in Paris: the gothic interior of Sainte Chapelle, with its elaborate stained-glass windows, and the interior of a discotheque, styled with colored lights and bright plastic elements. Both, though for different purposes, emphasize the relation between an architectural structure and its interior environment, as a place for people to congregate. When, some months later, Aurdal installed *Omgivelser* in the Kunstnernes Hus, its form was also devised to establish a social environment.

In 1972, Aurdal won a competition to make an outdoor sculpture for the yard of Trosterud Elementary School in Oslo, and made a group of structures using the same system of pipe segments she had used at the Kunstnernes Hus. Titled *Havbølger* (Ocean Waves), here it became a play structure for children to climb on: a formal and practical reconfiguration that suggested an expanded notion of the political through a redefinition of context, opening up the work's meaning and purpose to reach beyond the art environment and into a working social context. A further iteration was made for the 1979 Sculpture Biennial in Middelheim, Antwerp, this time a thirty-four-meter-long group of three sculptures. It was named *Greetings to the Lucas Workers* in a gesture of solidarity with the employees of Lucas Aerospace in the UK, who had proposed to switch from manufacturing arms to making medical equipment and sustainable energy technology. Each reconfiguration of her sculptural system emphasizes a different social connection, thereby insisting on context and audience as changeable but always implicated, and the work as an intrinsically political structure.

* * *

Little evidence remains of this sculpture's various early manifestations. In 1994 *Havbølger* was removed from Trosterud schoolyard due to damage; it was never repaired and was finally destroyed in 2008. Aurdal, too, slipped out of visibility, having begun teaching in Trondheim in 1975, and then suffering from health problems following an accident in her studio that took many years to recover from. Throughout the subsequent period, although she did not exhibit her work, the modular pipe form continued to occupy her. She constructed small cardboard models of the structures and used a Xerox machine to copy her drawings, which she reworked, copied, and reworked again, until no sense of original versus copy remained.

After Aurdal had spent several decades in obscurity, the Norwegian artist Eline Mugaas chanced upon a small documentary image of her 1969 Kunstnernes Hus sculpture. Mugaas sought her out and began to work with her, showing *Mobile* in a group show at Kunsthall Oslo in 2013, and putting together a richly illustrated book documenting Aurdal's archive and legacy. As Mugaas puts it, "I wanted to make her invisibility visible." While there have been vast sociopolitical, economic, and technological changes in the interim period of almost fifty years between the work's initial exhibition and its current installation in the Nordic Pavilion, what remains constant is the work's hospitable, even utopian aspect—its open invitation to participate. It occupies space, transforming it into a container and catalyst for contingent action. It *mobilizes*, and what could be more timely or essential than that?

Nina Canell

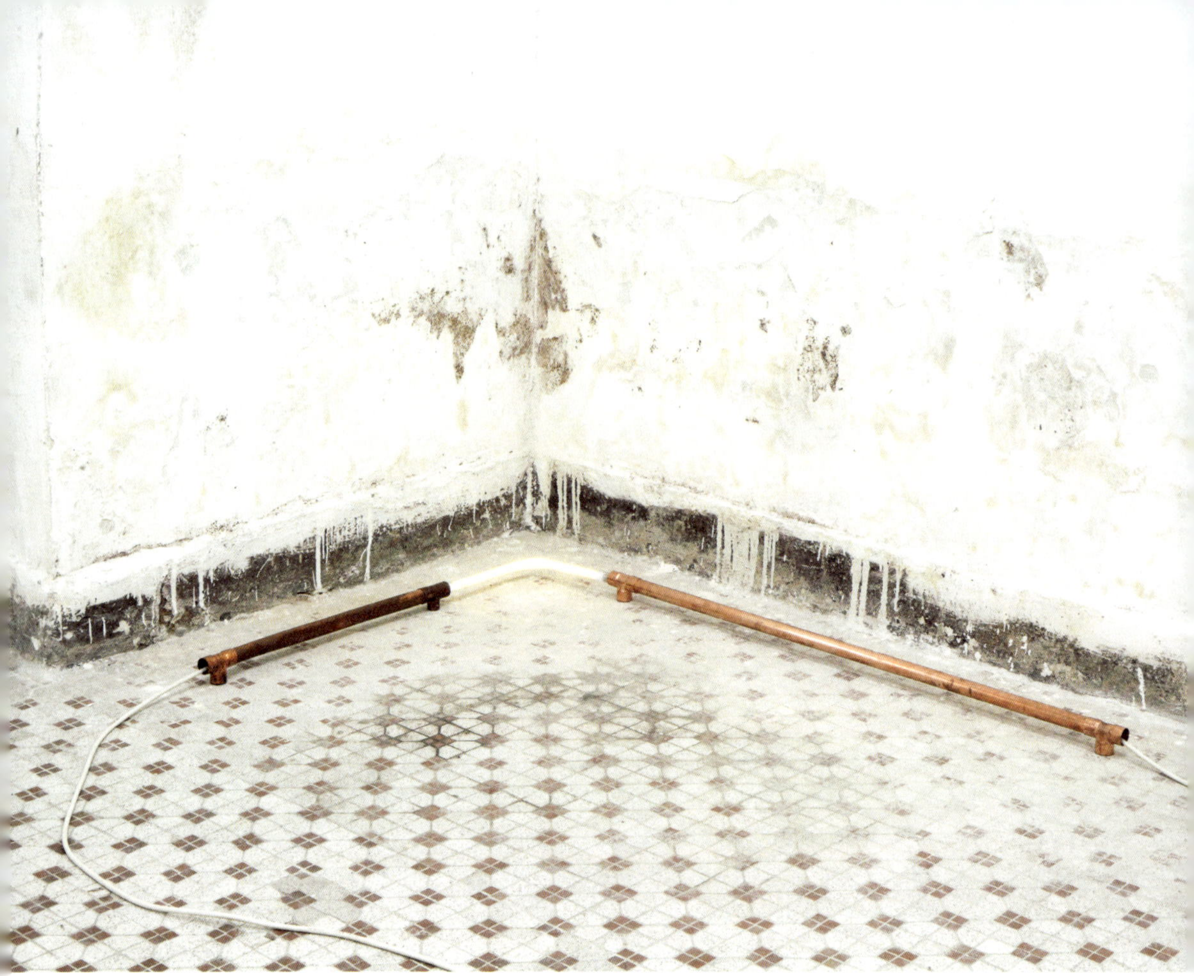

Soft Corner, 2013
Neon, copper, cable, 5000 volts
dimensions variable

Tip of the Tongue, 2016
Dictaphone, bouncy ball, silicone, paper, tape
18.5 × 11 × 4 cm

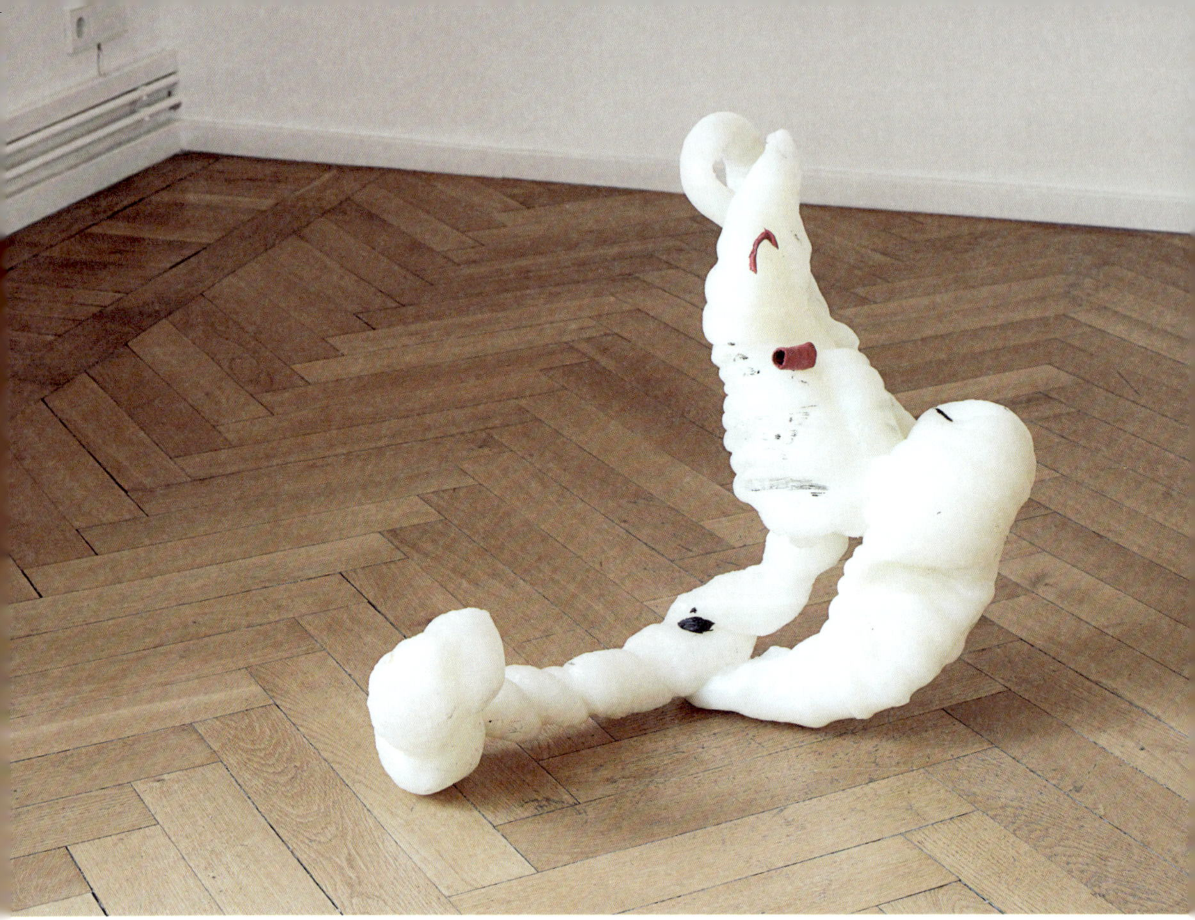

Shedding Sheaths (B), 2016
Fiber-optic cable sheaths
dimensions variable (detail)

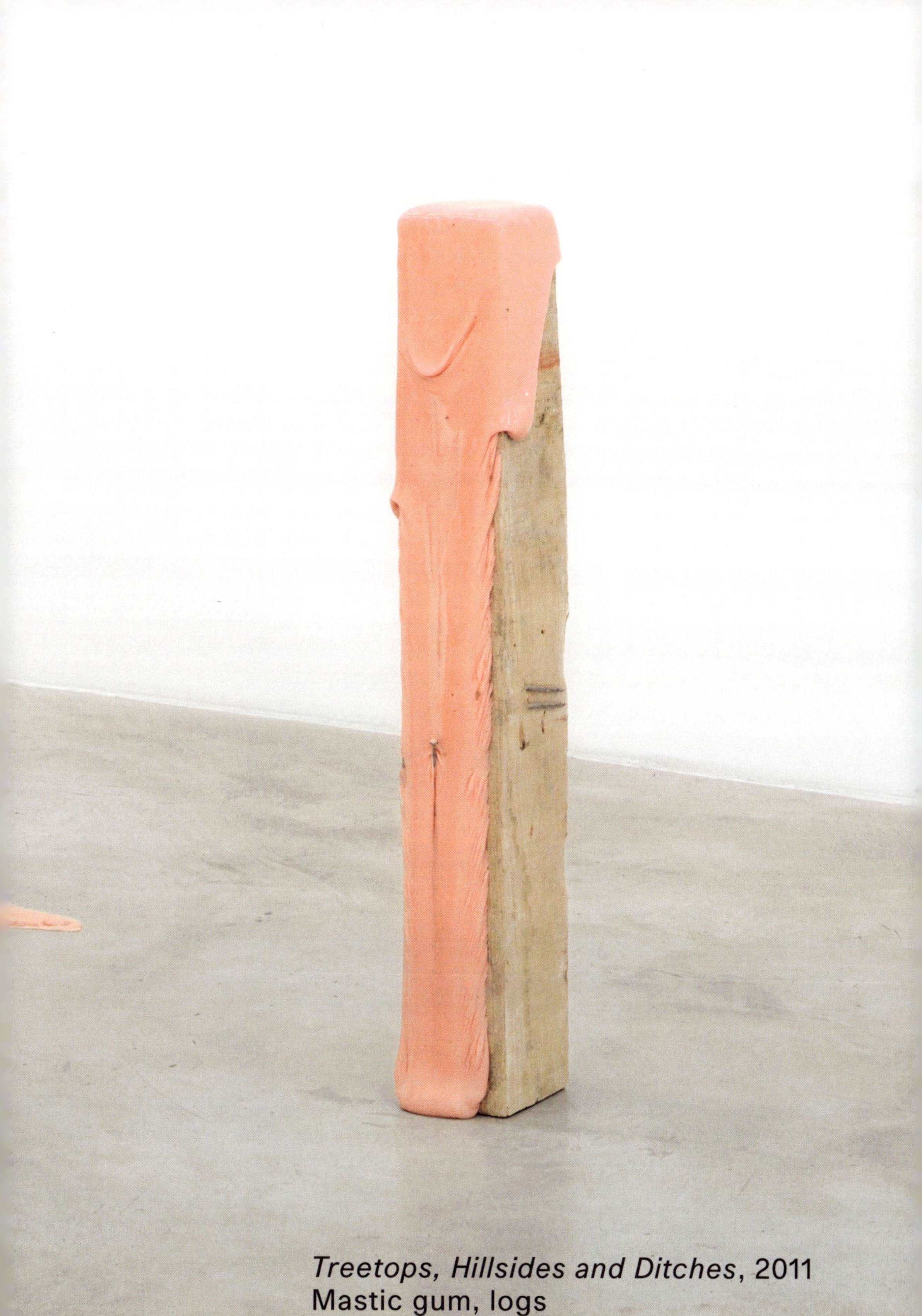

Treetops, Hillsides and Ditches, 2011
Mastic gum, logs
dimensions variable (detail)

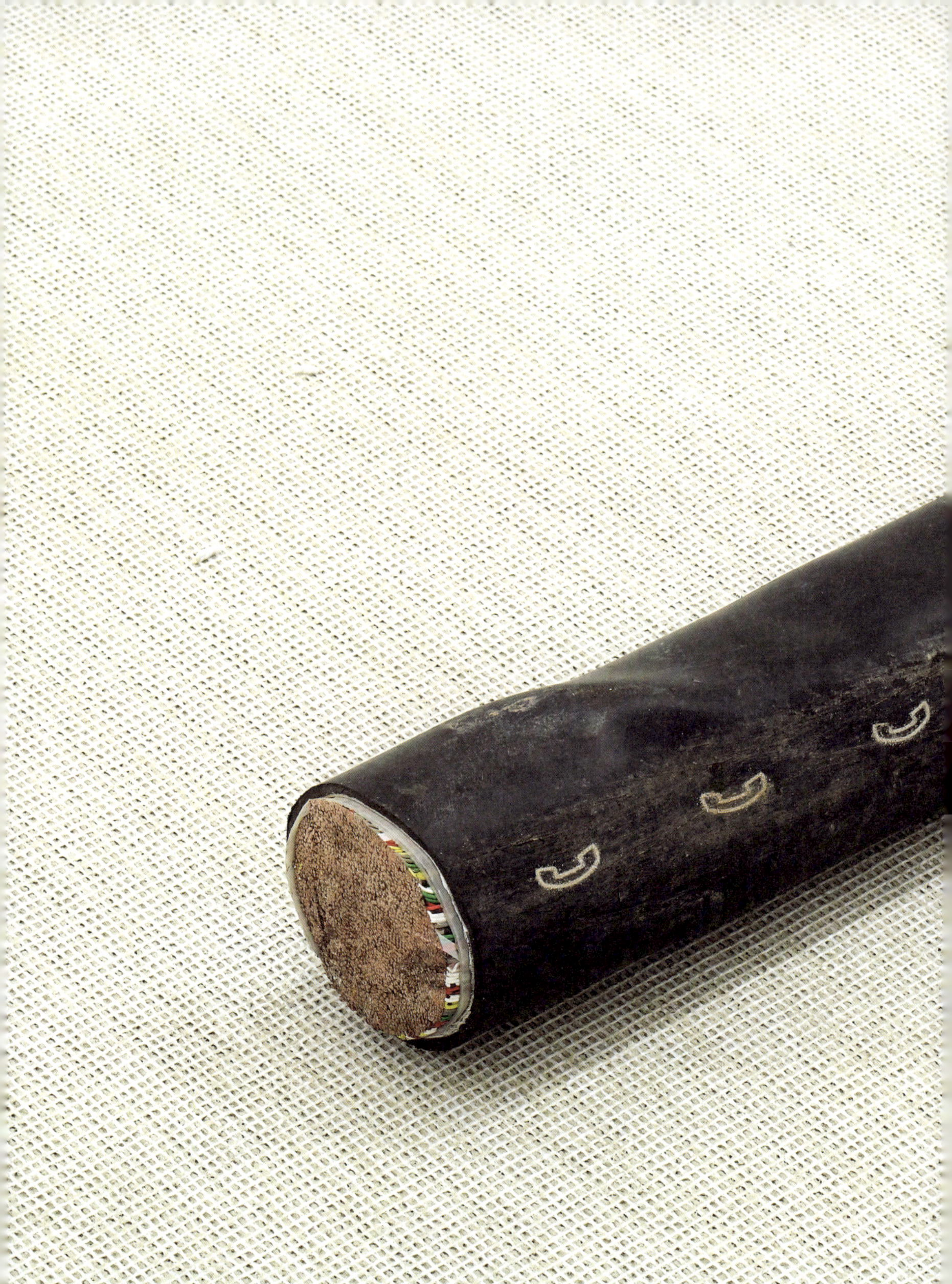

Brief Syllable (Flat), 2015
Telecommunication cable
10 × 197 × 159 cm

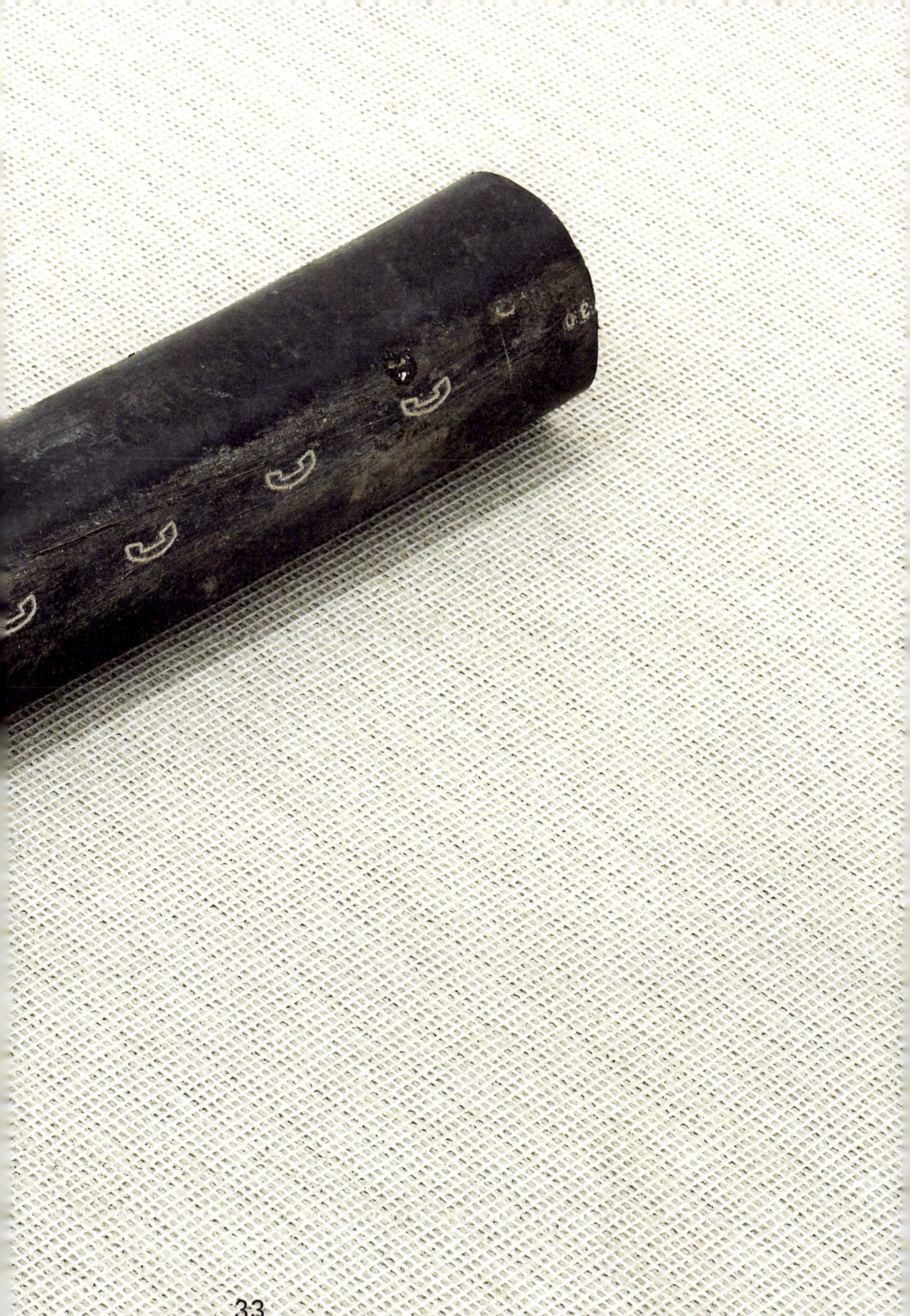

Relation Textures
by Chris Sharp

I have been looking at and thinking about Nina Canell's (b. 1979) work for the past six years on a relatively consistent basis. In this time period, and no doubt before, it has, to all intents and purposes, struck a pretty steady course, and yet it is constantly evolving. Essentially about more—much more—than meets the eye, Canell's work is interested in the in-between, micro-phenomena, the imperceptible, as well as conductors, or non-conductors, that might forcibly transform into conductors, and materials that might allow themselves to be thickened, if not thinned, into new material consistencies. These plastic, so to speak, preoccupations are pretty consistent throughout what she does, but how she thinks and speaks about them always seems to be moving toward greater and greater refinement.

The last time we discussed her work, we spoke about "free-space path loss," a phenomenon native to transmission terminology. It speaks to how a given signal erodes bit by bit until inevitably lost, as if through attrition, via the environment of encounters along its trajectory. This deterioration, aural or visual, embodies the modulation by intervening phenomena (e.g., a song by static or a mountain by mist), in such a way that it is not simply an interruption but also concerned with, in the artist's own words, "relational textures in and between objects." Similarly, where things change or morph into or under the influence of one another is where Canell finds her sculptural process of transformative affect. This is why you are liable to encounter so many omnidirectional conductors in her work, ranging from water to segments of subterranean fiber-optic cable, rows of nails, electric frequencies, and bouncing balls.

By the same token, Canell's work is either quite literally animated by a process, which may or may not be perceivable by human senses, or it has been the site of a process, in that an encounter or traversal has taken place. In the case of the former, I am thinking of her works with raw mastic gum that she began exhibiting in 2011, which consist of vertically positioned supports with pinkly pigmented gum spread over their uppermost extremities. Throughout the course of their exhibition, the highly viscous gum slowly and imperceptibly submits to gravity, oozing downward toward and across the floor. Natural sap from various trees has been chewed as gum since ancient times, used as glue and later as insulating material for early signaling cables. Like many works by Canell, the site of this piece is in the transience of the interaction of the materials themselves and the energy they produce.

More recently employed, and describing the process in which a traversal has already taken place in her work, are the synthetic skins of today's infrastructural nervous system, embodied by the installations *Shedding Sheaths* (2015–16). These consist of groupings of found and recuperated partially melted tangles of recycled fiber-optic cable sheaths. Some are fused together in serpentine piles, and others assume strange, almost muscle-like shapes, which curl and extend upward. Marked by a tactile organic quality, they are both sites and traces of energy, from the initial information and relations that coursed through their centers to the emptying out and removal of their inner cores. As such, the work is always the site of something happening or having happened. It testifies.

Despite the work's essentially indexical nature—the sense that it points to a pastness or a present that will eventually flow into the past—it is not necessarily melancholic or elegiac. This is not to say that the work is devoid of these aspects; as per its various registrations of loss, this reading is inevitable, and necessarily tempers it with a touch of allegory. But more important than this is its capacity to move in unexpected directions. Indeed, if there is any mood to the work, it is a complex admixture of genuine curiosity, sustained and directed attention, a love of precision, a will to be informed, and a state of pure, if rigorous, openness.

For all its underpinnings and interest, no amount of language can alternatively transmit or resolve what Canell makes. In other words, no matter how many words you throw at her objects, they will never surrender their essential enigmatic constitution, which is as inseparable from the materials she uses as it is from how they are formalized. She is interested in what sculpture has been and what it can be—not to mention *how* it can be (more often than not, quite literally bent into hum and hiss). Thus while her work can easily be co-opted by discourses of research and so-called knowledge production, its real traction lies elsewhere: not in its capacity to explain or solve the world but in rendering it more dense, not to mention palpable with its own impurities. Thus it is at once timely and timeless. The latter because it is dealing with the same thing that sculptors have always dealt with: form, material, and three dimensions, as well as, in her case, the fourth dimension. The former because at a moment when instantaneous communication and transmission of information are taken for granted, her work and its preoccupation with the alleged and ultimately mythical immateriality of the contemporary world takes nothing for granted.

Charlotte Johannesson

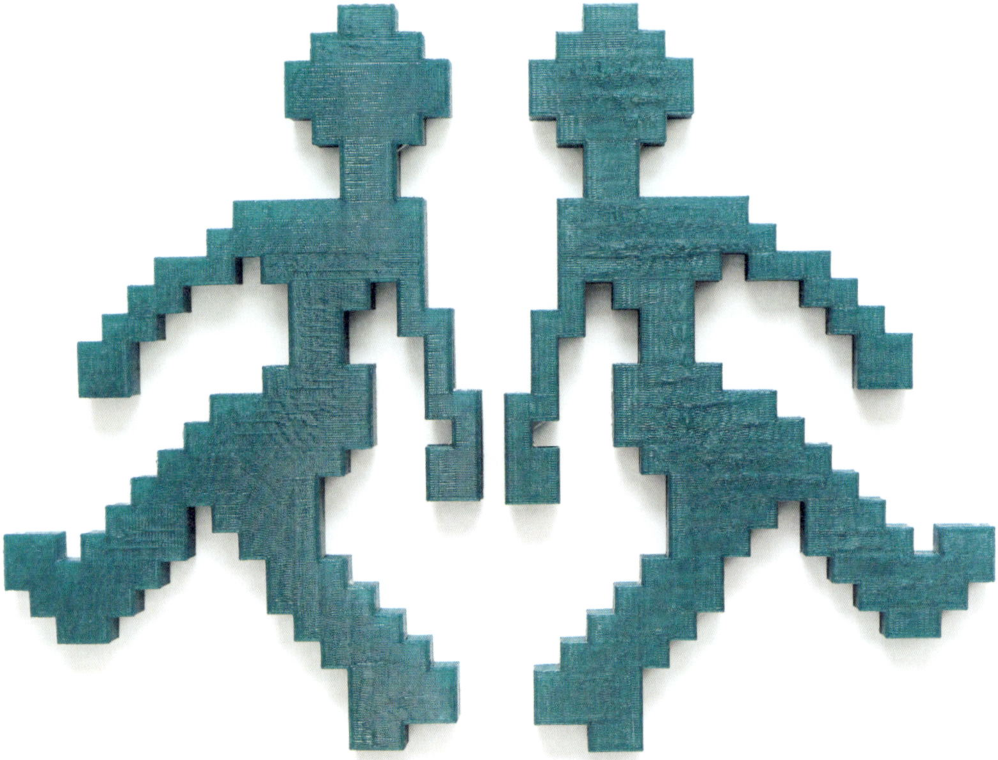

Human Figure, 2017
3D print

24 × 26 × 1 cm

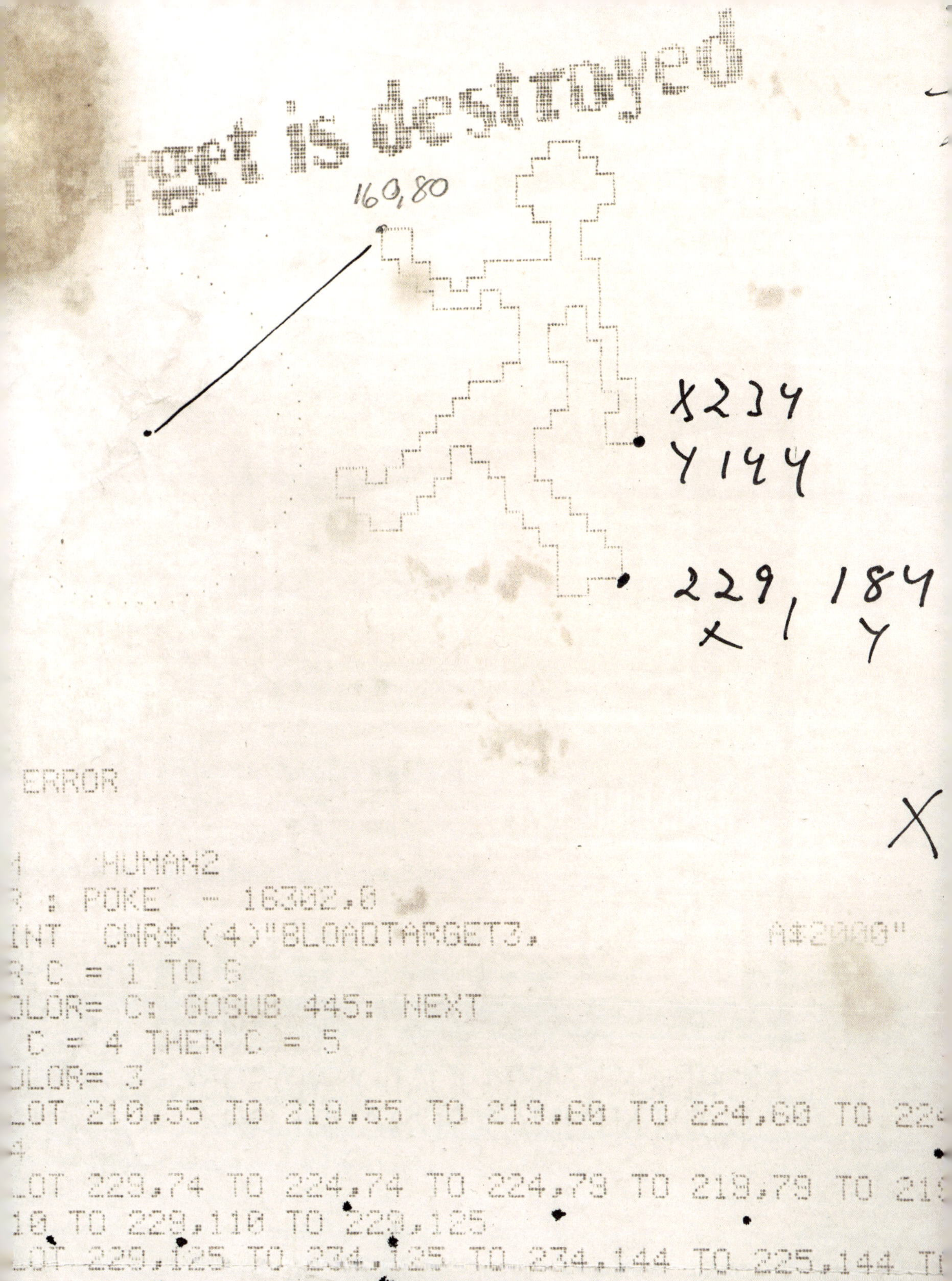

Untitled, 1983
Basic computer program
30 × 50 cm

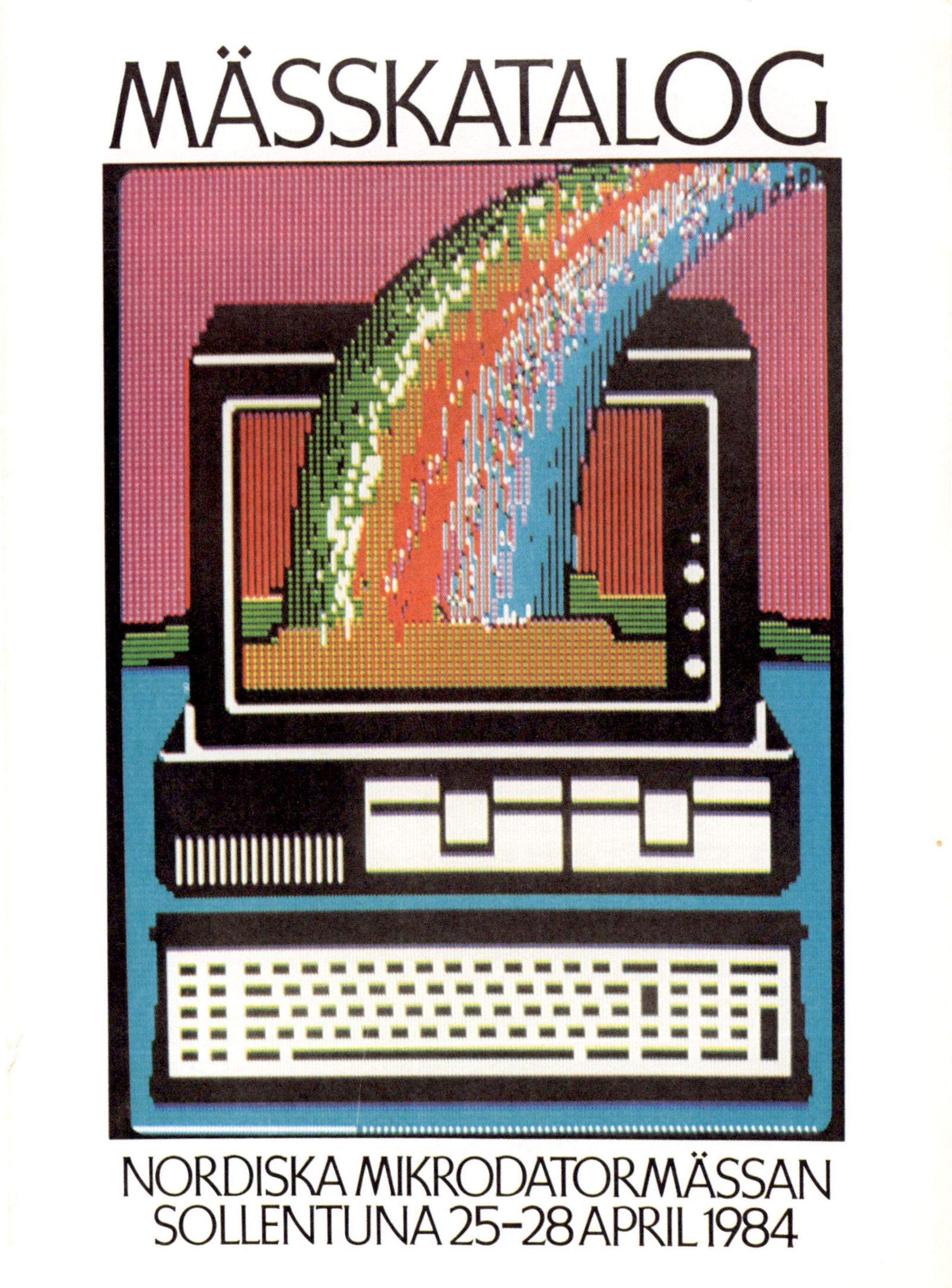

Commission for poster
and catalogue cover, 1984
28.5 × 21.3 cm

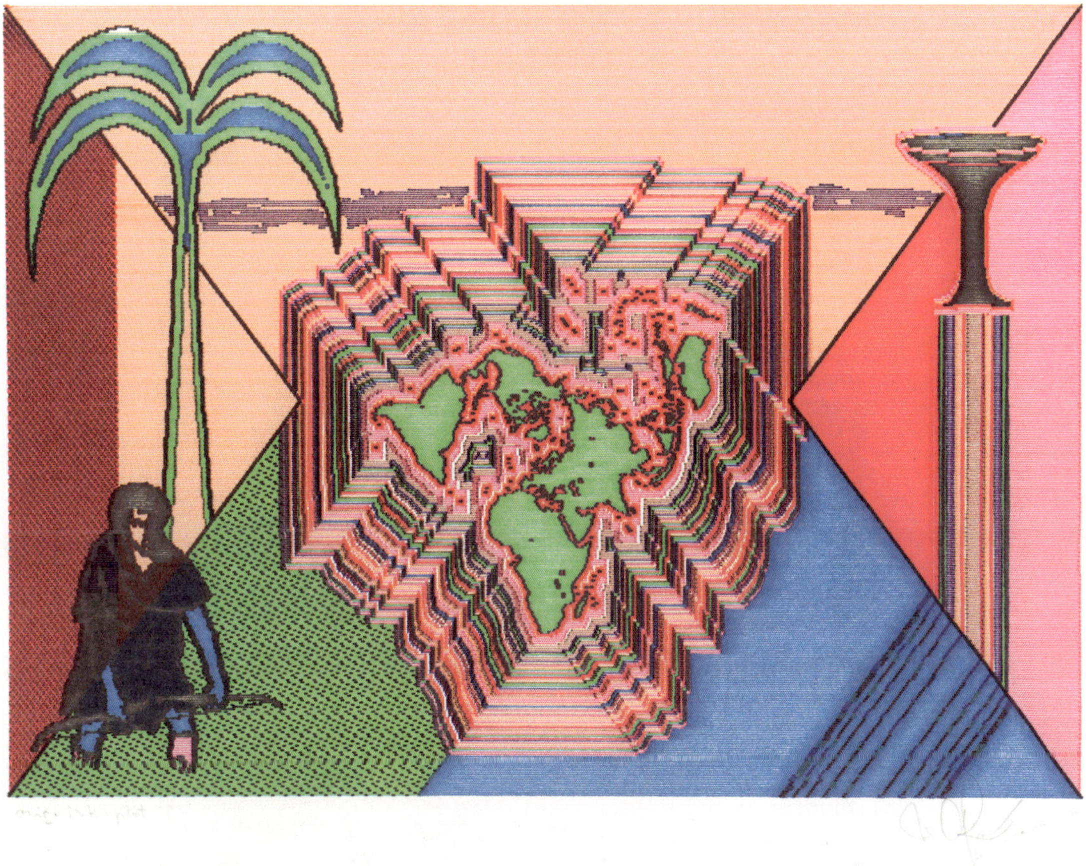

Original Computer Graphics Art (Parsifal),
1981–86
Apple II computer (the Digital Theatre)
19 × 27 cm

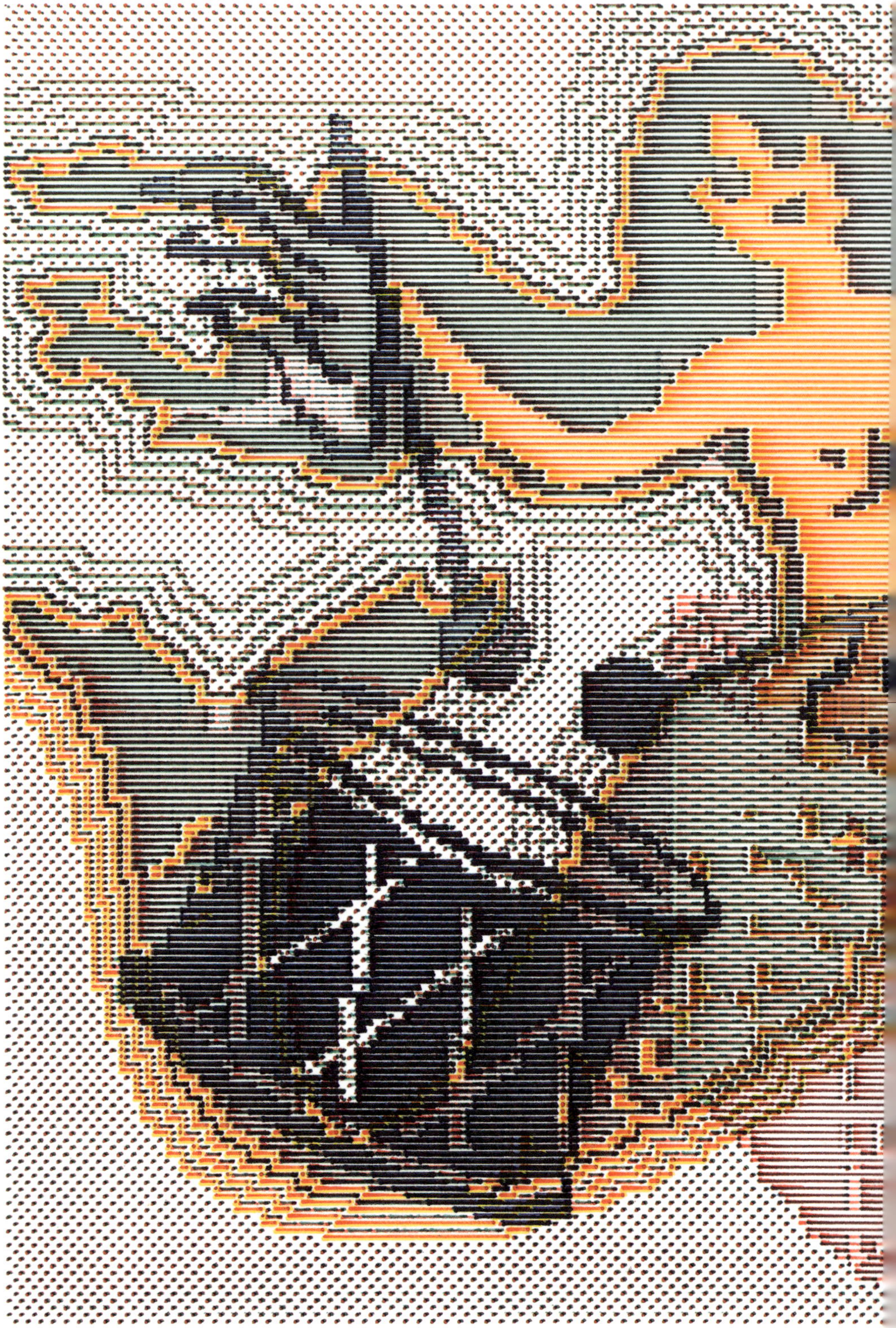

Original Computer Graphics Art
(Vote for Me), 1983
Apple II computer (the Digital Theatre)
29.7 × 42 cm

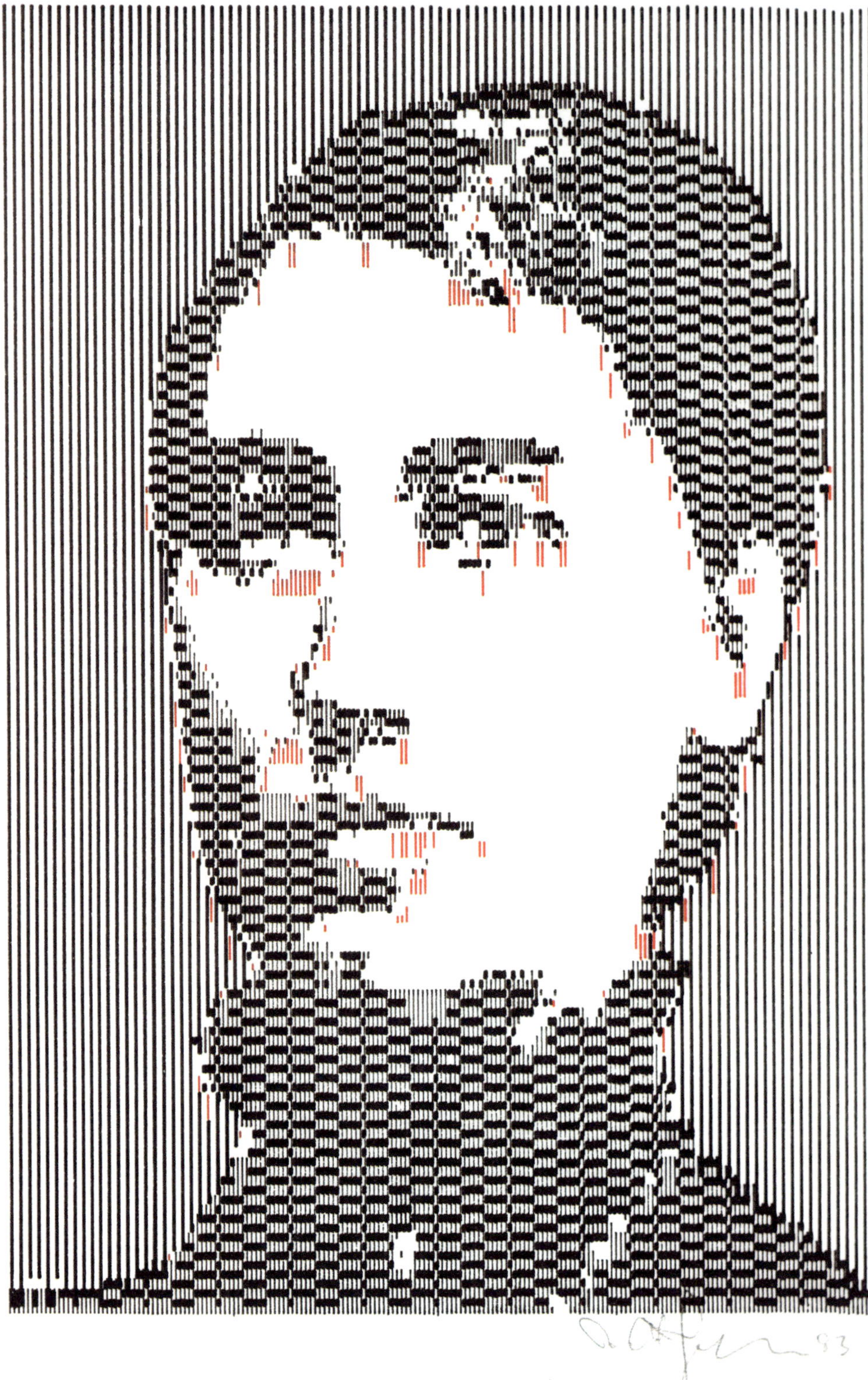

Original Computer Graphics Art
(Victoria Benedictsson), 1983
Apple II computer (the Digital Theatre)
17 × 12 cm

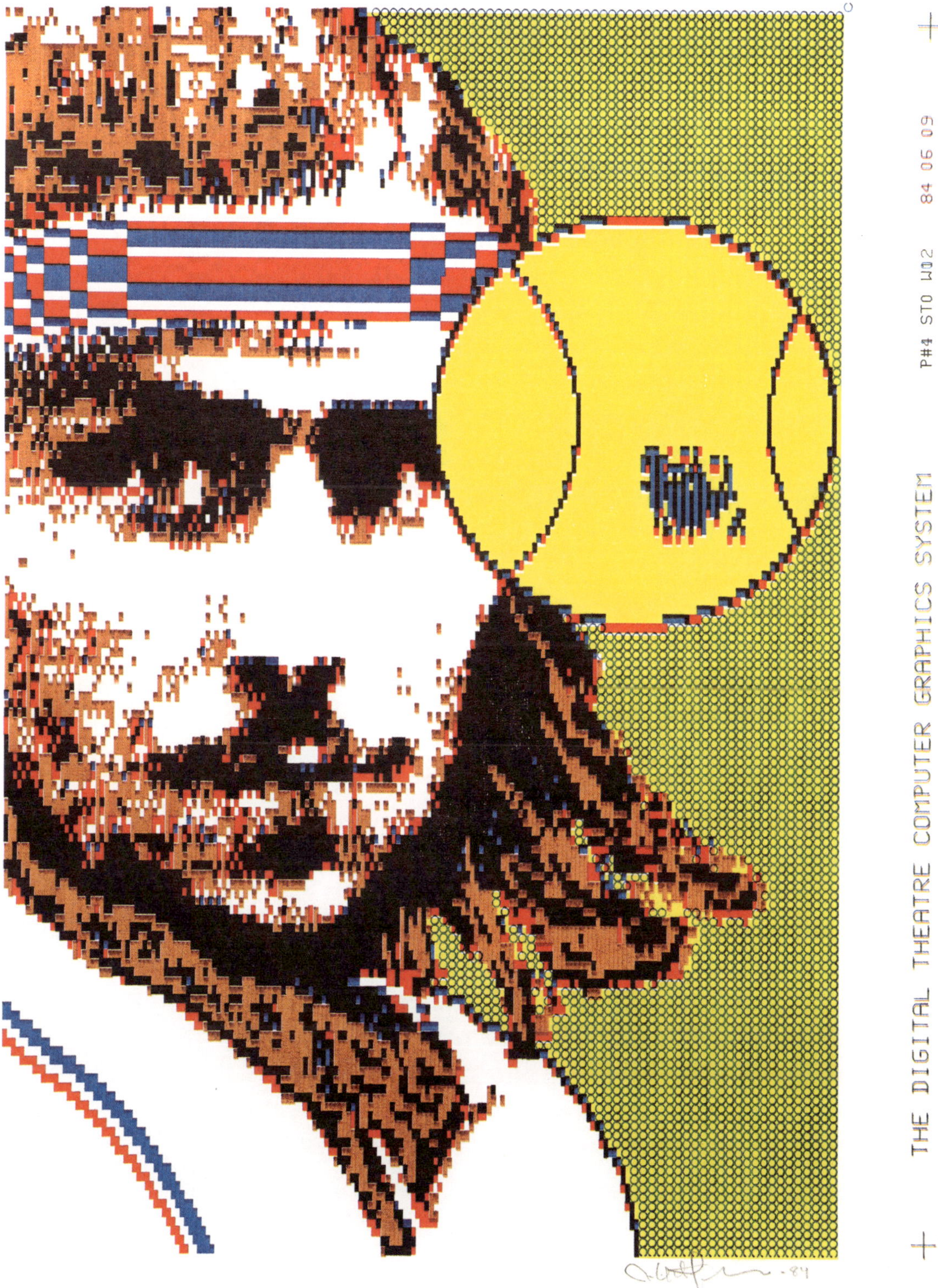

Original Computer Graphics Art (Björn Borg), 1983
Apple II computer (the Digital Theatre)
17 × 12 cm

I'm No Angel: Charlotte Johannesson
by Cecilia Widenheim

How has computer code shaped contemporary culture? How do we make sense of the interplay between art and the technical, economic, social, and political changes of our time? And is the history of technology exclusively a patriarchal matter? Recently the Faculty of Engineering at Lund University in Sweden held a hackathon in memory of Ada Lovelace, the nineteenth-century female mathematician who is often considered the world's first computer programmer. Around the world every year in mid-October, she is honored in various ways on Ada Lovelace Day.

The relationship between computer code and textile craft is one of the keys to Charlotte Johannesson's (b. 1943) aesthetic world and her interest in contemporary image production–the image produced by digital technology. In the 1960s she started Cannabis, a weaving workshop in Malmö named for the cannabis plant from which the hemp fibers she used in her weaving are derived. Between 1962 and 1964 she took a number of weaving courses in Malmö and learned the basics of this increasingly marginalized textile handicraft. What most fascinated her was the planning of advanced patterns on graph paper and mastering the techniques that women in southern Sweden had turned into a pure art form over the course of centuries, for instance *krabbasnår* brocading, *dukagång* and *opphämta*'s supplementary weft structure, and *rosengång* (rose path) and *munkabälte* (monk's belt) patterns.

Johannesson's sense of systematics and knowledge of the logic of the production process provided the basis for the development of her multilayered artistry; she became a unique voice in Nordic artistic life from the 1960s onward. In many ways her work is pioneering. Years later the warp and woof of weaving, with its vertical and horizontal lines as a composition principle, proved more or less directly translatable into computing languages. It wasn't a big step, according to the artist. With his punch-card loom around 1800, the Frenchman Jean Marie Jacquard had already begun to conceive of modern computing, in that the holes in each punched card guided how the warp was drawn through, for every throw the weaver made with the shuttle.

At the weaving courses she attended, Johannesson realized she wanted to use weaving techniques for a more contemporary image production. She wanted to involve society beyond the hand weaver's workshop, and create weaves charged with meaning.

And so were born a number of works in which ancient weaving techniques and a culture of craftsmanship met the radical politics of the day and buzzword-like messages: *Terror* (1978), *Attack* (1978), *New Wave* (1977), *No Future* (1977), and *Achtung!* (1975). The German Red Army Faction meets the flying ace of the American cartoon *Peanuts* in *Frei Die Raf* (Free RAF, 1976). High meets low. A major source of inspiration was the textile artist Hannah Ryggen, also a Malmö native. With her politically and socially conscious compositions, Ryggen transformed tradition-heavy decorative weaving into an expressive and full-feathered visual art.

Johannesson's weaves attest to a postmodern way of thinking, but also to a consciously feminist stance along with apparent influences from the punk movement of the time. Several of her weaves are penetrated with metal objects—sewing needles and extra-large safety pins or pencil sharpeners. Several of them have been fitted with a lintel in the form of a saw blade or a floor mop. During these years Johannesson unlocked a way of composing that she would further develop in her computer-generated images. A recurring image in her visual world is the stick-figure man fleeing in every direction—from war, confrontation, the outposts of power. Fittingly enough, one of these compositions is called *Run for Your Life* (1978).

The present day was literally being woven into textile after textile. The 1973 military coup d'état against democratically elected Chilean president Salvador Allende was the starting point for a textile called *Chile Echoes in My Skull* (1973). The large 1977 tapestry *Drop Dead* was a comment on the hydrogen bomb and its ability to annihilate that is as efficient as it is inhuman. The same year, Johannesson and her partner, Sture Johannesson, interviewed the Sex Pistols' front man Johnny Rotten in Växjö. The Sex Pistols had just released the single "God Save the Queen," and the first question they had for the legendary punk rocker was about Berlin and the Baader-Meinhof's latest actions. The year 1977 was one of upheaval, and a series of dramatic events in Germany rattled the surrounding world. But soon Charlotte and Sture would turn their gaze in a completely different direction: the world of computers and the United States, where that same year the American military had christened their new programming language "ADA" in honor of Ada Lovelace, the mother of the algorithm.

In 1978 Johannesson decided to trade one of her large tapestries, *I'm No Angel* (1973), for an Apple II Plus personal computer, one of the first on the market. This signaled the start of a new artistic journey. Sture Johannesson had already been in contact with IBM in the 1960s, and when the first computers with monitors began to appear, the couple built the Digital Theatre in Malmö, one of the first computer graphics studios in Europe. Photographs show the impressive computer landscape that filled an entire Malmö apartment from 1981 to 1985. Trips to the American West Coast and interactions with key figures in the early computer industry, such as Steve Wozniak, the genius behind the Apple II and Steve Jobs's partner, and Sten Kallin at IBM in Sweden, gave rise to a unique network for these two Swedish artists. The images that Charlotte Johannesson was composing at this time were built up as collages of fragments and details that were then printed out, often in bright, strong colors against a black background. They were made of picture elements or *pixels*: a word invented in the 1960s to describe video images in conjunction with space travels. But computer technology was still in its infancy then. The lack of programs for the production of images opened up a space for experimentation and expressions of a hitherto unknown aesthetic: the art of computer-generated imagery.

Johannesson saw that a weaving draft could be translated into pixels in the digital world—239 pixels wide and 191 pixels high. Her predilection for world maps and images of Earth as seen from space underscore the universal, visionary quality of the screenprint series. Hannah

Ryggen's monumental 1956 work *We Live on a Star* comes to mind, a work that described humankind's vulnerability in a world marked by rearmament. The World Wide Web was at the door. Details that refer to specific historical events, such as the Falklands War, create the impression that in the 1980s Johannesson had managed to connect to a global link where the mass media's flood of images was flowing, anticipating the Internet.

Looking back at the works from this period, one also finds a series of more abstract compositions in a slightly softer color scale, and a series of vivid portraits. It's the visual culture of the 1980s, featuring icons such as David Bowie, Bob Dylan, Boy George, Lech Walesa, and Björn Borg, as well as more unexpected imagery. There are, for instance, personalities such as Ahmad Shah Massoud, the Afghan resistance leader, also known as "the man who won the Cold War." Another portrait draws from a photograph of Victoria Benedictsson, the legendary author from Skåne in southern Sweden who used a male pseudonym, Ernst Ahlgren, to be able to publish her radical texts. At the age of thirty-eight she took her own life in protest of the stifling gender hierarchy of the late 1800s.

The view of the individual in an ever more globalized world and the view of the personal in the shadow of the Cold War are recurring themes in a number of Johannesson's textiles that show up later in her computer-generated works. The themes are in many ways compatible with the Digital Theatre as an idea and method of production. The artist's personal identity number and fingerprints appear in numerous images, a direct commentary on the dehumanized view of modern humanity, registered as a number. When personal identity numbers started to be managed by computers in the 1960s, a tenth number was introduced, the checksum.

A look back at Charlotte Johannesson's works yields priceless knowledge about the interplay between art and the technological developments of our time. The Digital Theatre staged the idea of a new industrial visual culture long before the term Industry 4.0 was used and long before analysts realized that the next industrial revolution—after steam power, the conveyor belt, and robots—would come in the form of a digital revolution.

Jumana Manna

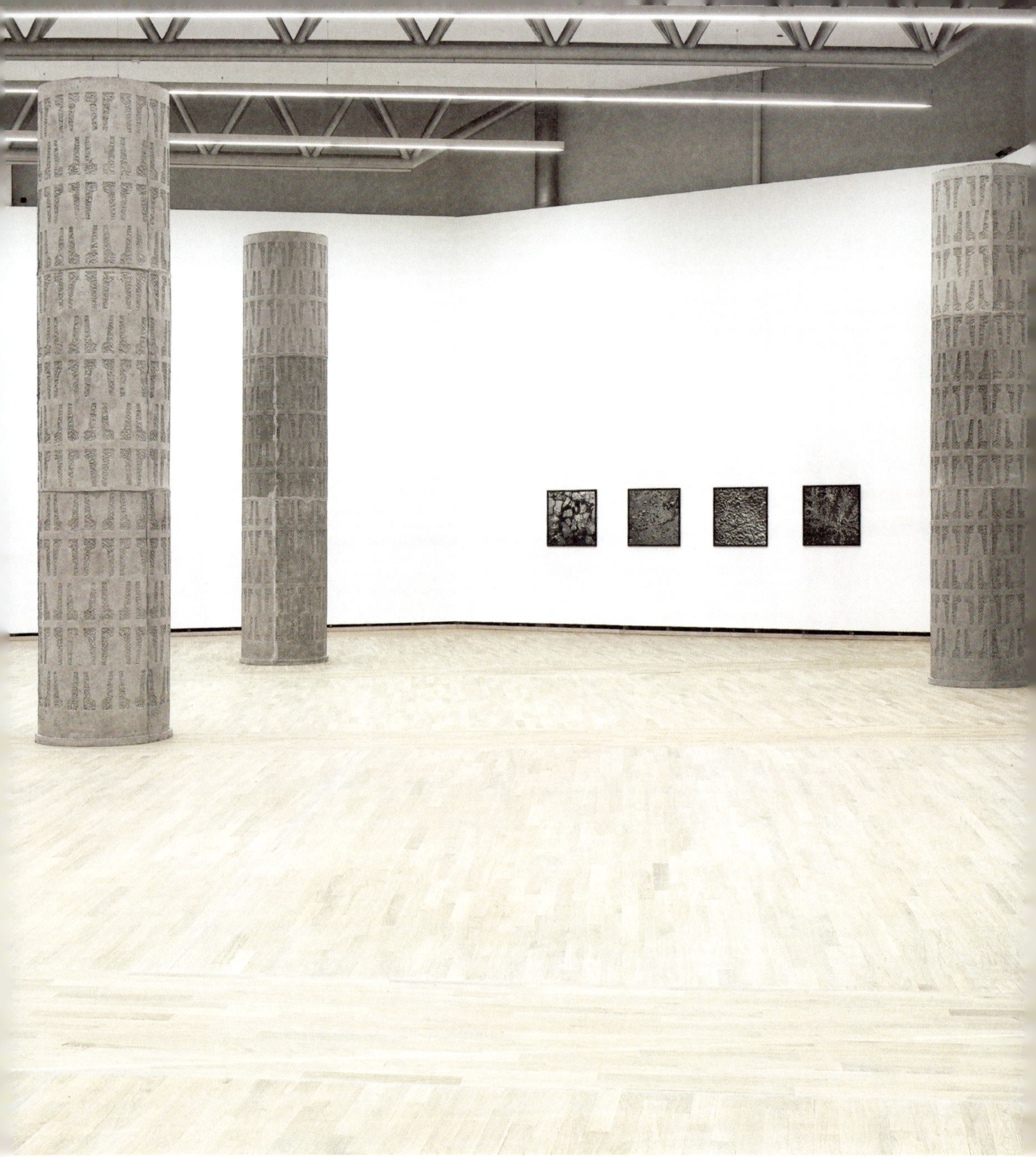

Government Quarter Study
Installation view, Henie Onstad
Kunstsenter, Høvikodden, 2014

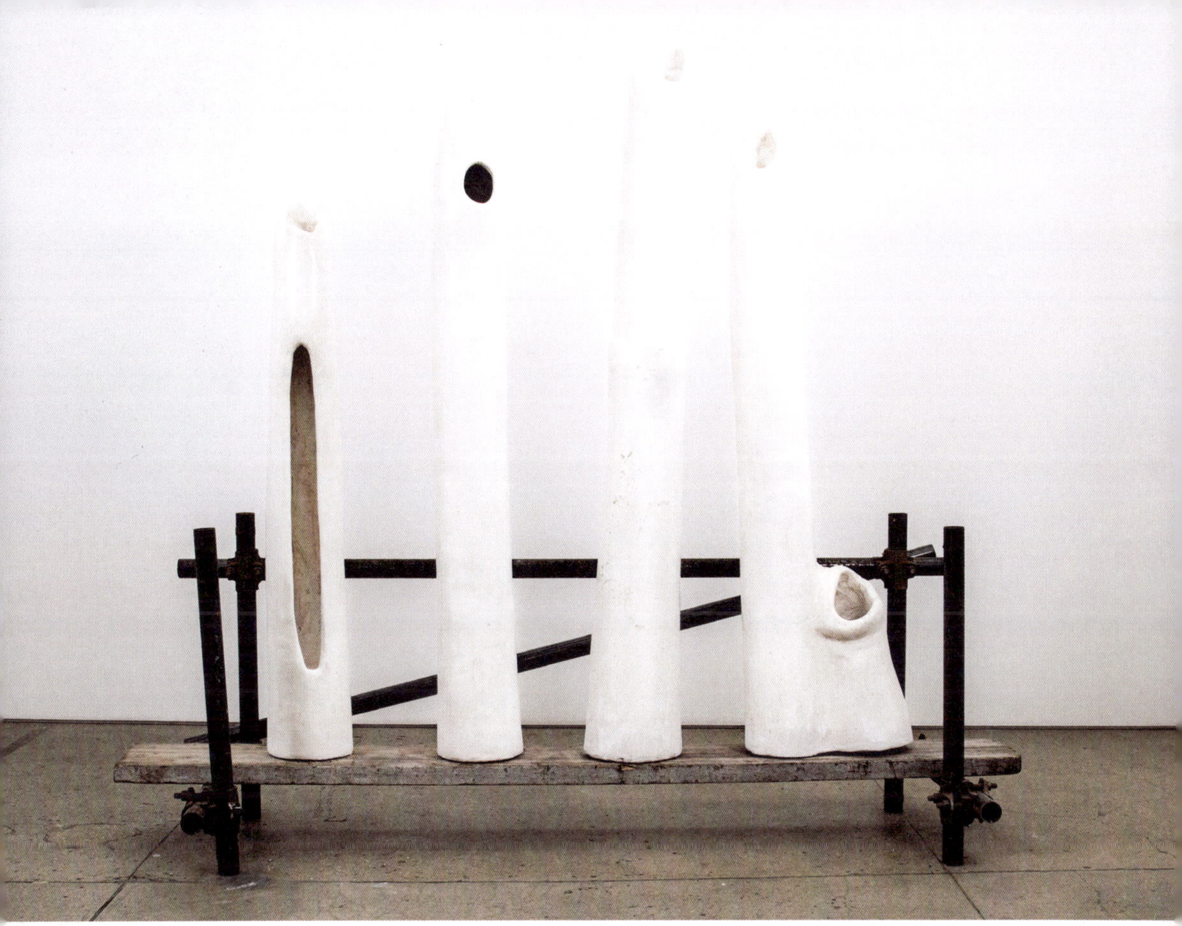

Amulet, 2016
Plaster, fiber, lacquer, metal scaffold, wood
170 × 150 × 40 cm

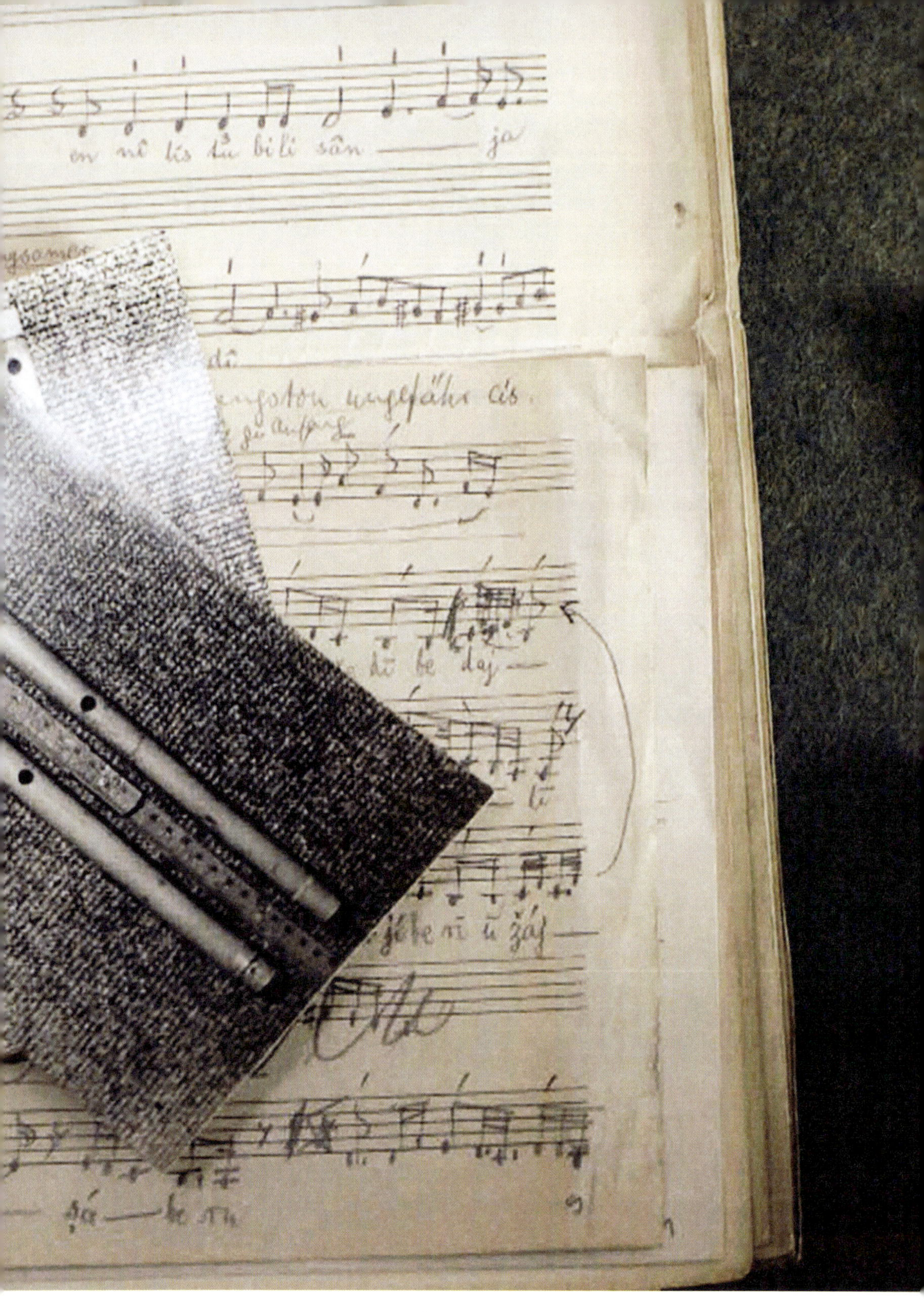

A Magical Substance Flows into Me, 2015
Still from 68 min HD video

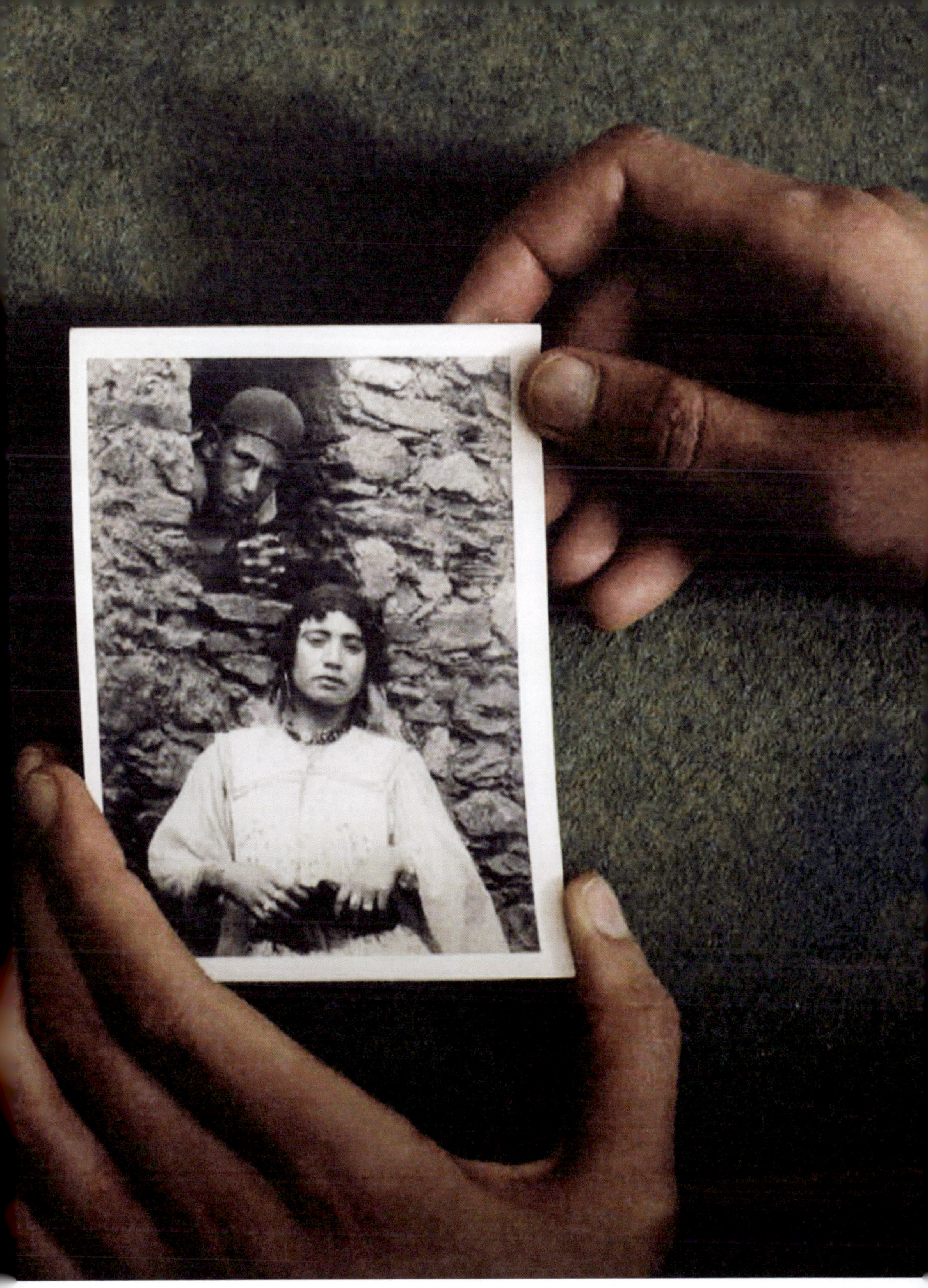

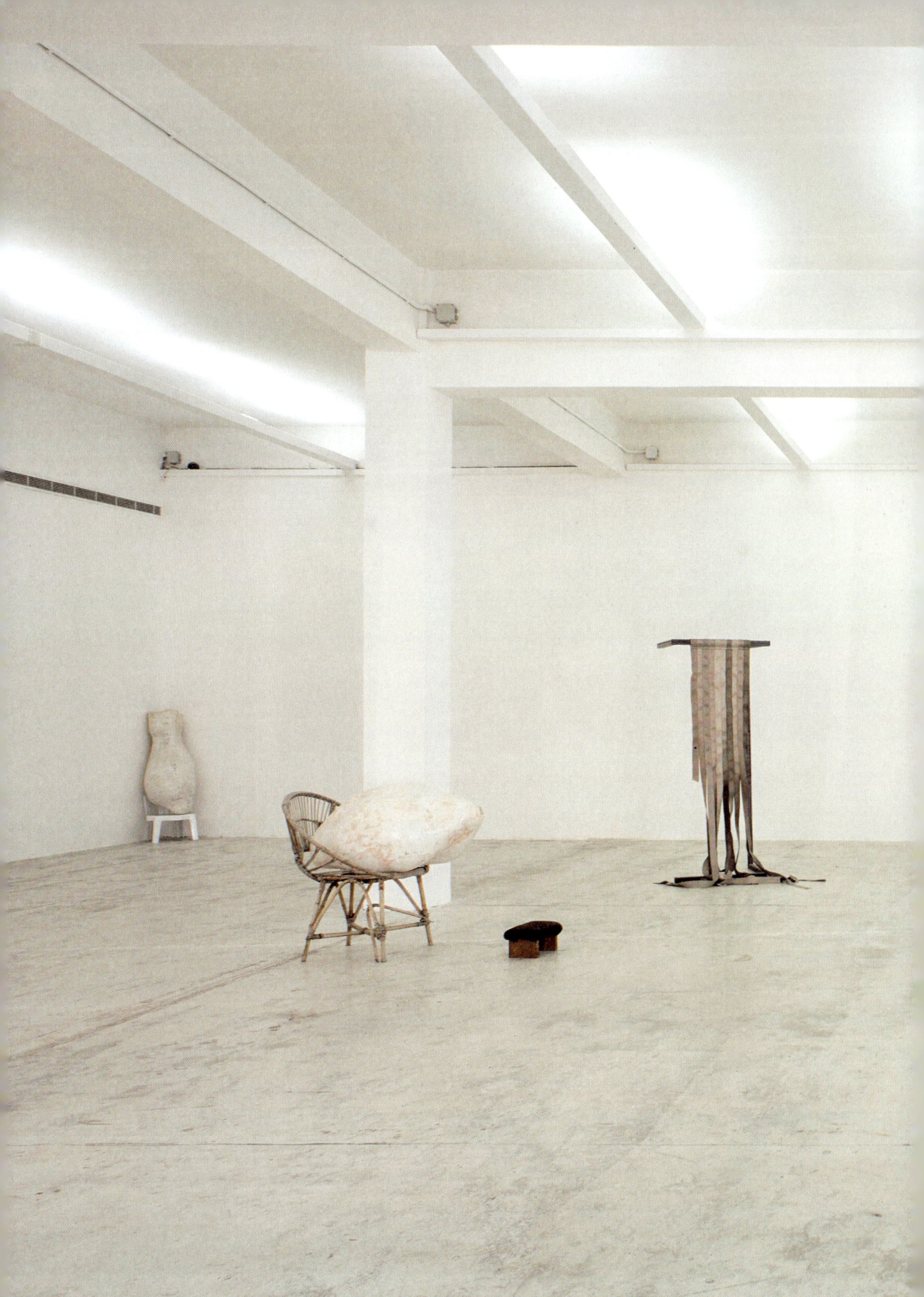

Aftercinema
Installation view, Beirut Art Center, 2015

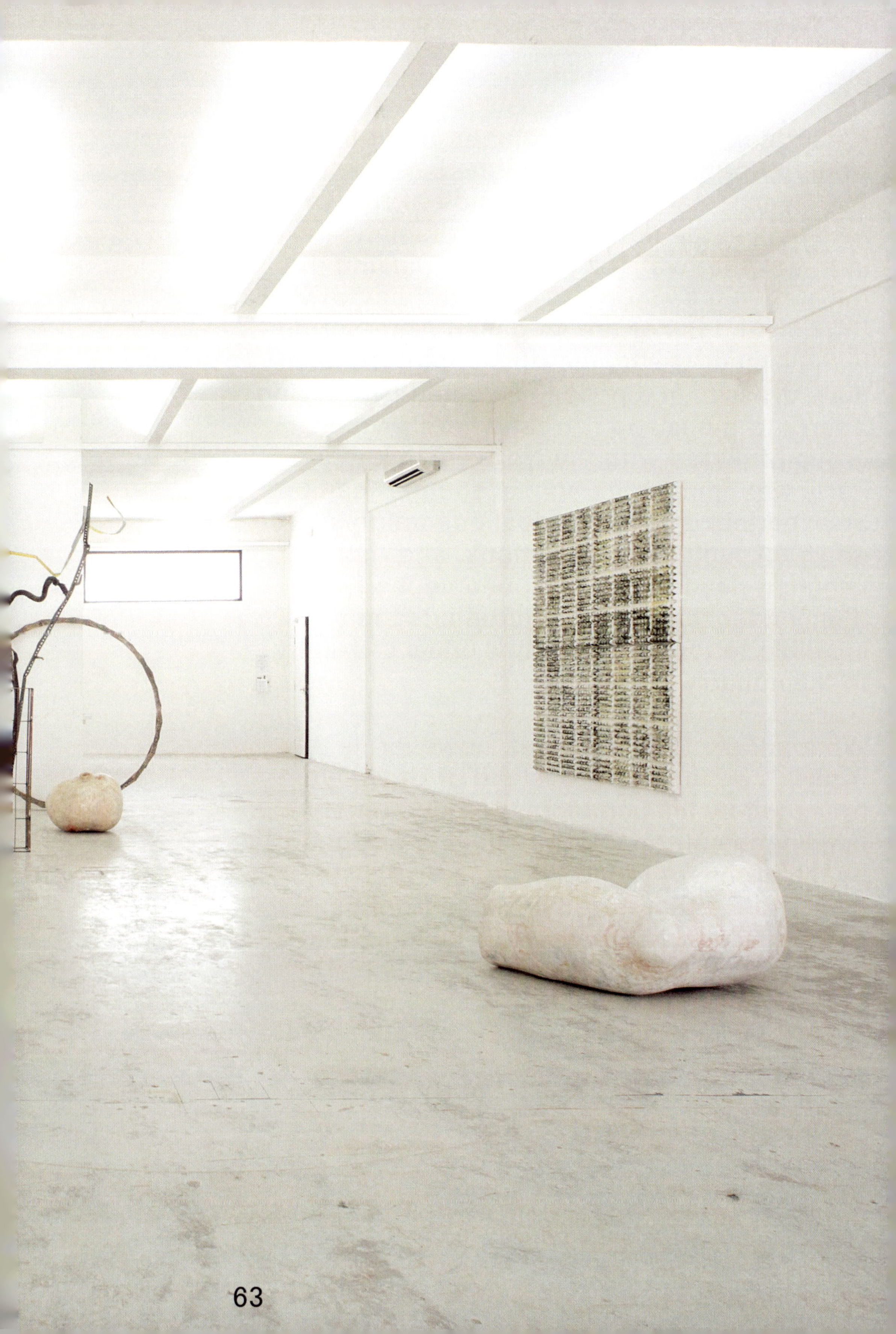

Jumana Manna
by Kaelen Wilson-Goldie

What people tend to remember about the Anders Breivik massacre in the summer of 2011—particularly people outside of Norway who took in the news of these traumatic events in a year that was full of them, including the full arc from euphoria to devastation that was the rise and fall of the so-called Arab Spring—is the island. The image of a young, troubled man, dressed in a policeman's uniform, taking a ferry to the island retreat where a youth group affiliated with the Norwegian Labor Party was running its annual summer camp, an experience of ideological education shared down through the generations, and then shooting dead sixty-seven people, half of them under the age of eighteen, is too indelible to forget, no matter one's proximity to the country itself.

What people tend to forget, however, is that Breivik's actions on the island of Utøya were preceded by his bombing of a government building in central Oslo, a building designed by the architect Erling Viksjø, a Brutalist masterpiece that mixed pebbles from nearby riverbeds into the concrete, a building that was meant to reflect the values of social democracy and the welfare state and did so, in part, by incorporating ornamentation and modernist artworks—Pablo Picasso murals, a Hannah Ryggen tapestry—into the design of the space itself. Eight people died in the bomb blast, and the highly symbolic building, home to the prime minister's office and the Ministry of Justice at the time, was heavily damaged. It wasn't destroyed. But it was left without its government function and consigned to an ambiguous role in the space between monument, memorial, and ruin.

The work of the Palestinian artist Jumana Manna (b. 1987) often shows her interest in the things that are forgotten, unexamined, or hidden in plain sight. Her carefully composed films and wilder assemblages of sculptural objects often take up the strange or unusual details that history leaves behind, the artifacts or anecdotes or even the uncomfortable facts that have been discarded either because they complicate the story or fit awkwardly in the way such a story is being told, revisited, and revised. These include a radio show on Oriental music made by the German ethnomusicologist Robert Lachmann in Palestine in the 1930s, which was a starting point for Manna's magisterial, feature-length film *A Magical Substance Flows into Me* (2015). They also include an archival portrait of the crowd at a masquerade ball in the port city of Jaffa in 1924, which is shown alongside Manna's *A Sketch of Manners (Alfred Roch's*

Last Masquerade) (2013), a twelve-minute video that brings the date up to 1942, moves the event to the famous American Colony Hotel in Jerusalem, and casts it as the last-ever masquerade ball in Mandate Palestine, allowing viewers, in turn, to imagine a time of decadence and androgyny, of nothing being quite so black and white, and then to feel the shock of that moment vanishing. Likewise, an herbarium at the American University of Beirut, established by a Protestant missionary in the nineteenth century who was intent on assembling scientific knowledge of Biblical lands, and which, in an installation by Manna in 2016, traces the movement of plant specimens, religious fervor, and the tropes of European painting through the systems and mechanisms of colonial power. And most recently, the subject of a film in progress, following the sensitive reconstitution in Lebanon's Bekaa Valley of a seed bank in Aleppo, thought to be intact but now totally inaccessible due to the Syrian civil war.

Manna was born in the United States and raised in Jerusalem. If her childhood was marked by the first intifada, then her adolescence was colored by the Oslo Accords and their aftermath, namely, the collapse of a revolutionary movement into petty politics, corruption, and graft, and the impossibility of a truly peaceful resolution to the Arab–Israeli conflict. Much of her work involves a search for some kind of evidence of the complexity of historical Palestine, which then becomes the basis for imagining another Palestine altogether. Along the way, Manna invokes other kinds of imaginings: religious, colonial, national, ideological, scientific, philanthropic, literary, cinematic—all seemingly out of a genuine interest in picking apart how the mythology of a people or a place is made. And while the majority of Manna's life and work centers on Jerusalem as a city with the most mythic imagination of them all, she also studied in Norway and lived there for years, returning often and making a number of key works exploring some of the unexpected links between the two places.

The Goodness Regime (2013), a twenty-one-minute video that Manna made in collaboration with the artist Sille Storihle, delves into Norway's many foundational narratives, from its role in the Crusades to its reaction to Nazi occupation in World War II to the status of its oil and gas industries and its reputation for being a just and benevolent broker of world peace, a good actor on the global stage, and a kind benefactor for developing countries. Using cherubic child actors to enact different episodes in both Norwegian and Palestinian history—including the handshake of Yasser Arafat and Yitzhak Rabin on the White House lawn in 1993—the film pans back and forth, from olive groves to snowstorms, nationalistic songs to a New Year's address on the inheritance of benevolence and solidarity, to consider how the elements of a national identity, narrative, and myth can come together in one instance and fall apart in another.

Government Quarter Study (2014) consists of three full-size casts of the lobby pillars from Erling Viksjø's bombed-but-not-destroyed building in Oslo, paired with four photographs by the British artist Mark Boyle (intensely close-up, abstract studies of blood, sweat, piss, and tears). Where the originals are solid and bear the load of the building, Manna's casts are hollow, constructed in pieces, with seams and imperfections. The sandblasted ornamentation that was characteristic of Viksjø's design comes across hauntingly well in her reproduction, lending the work an extremely subtle, almost coded sensitivity, bringing many different and often bombastic acts and gestures—nation building, ideological construction, mythmaking, art making, violence, attack, destruction—down to the imagined touch of a fingertip on stones revealed in concrete.

69 Kaelen Wilson-Goldie

Pasi “Sleeping” Myllymäki

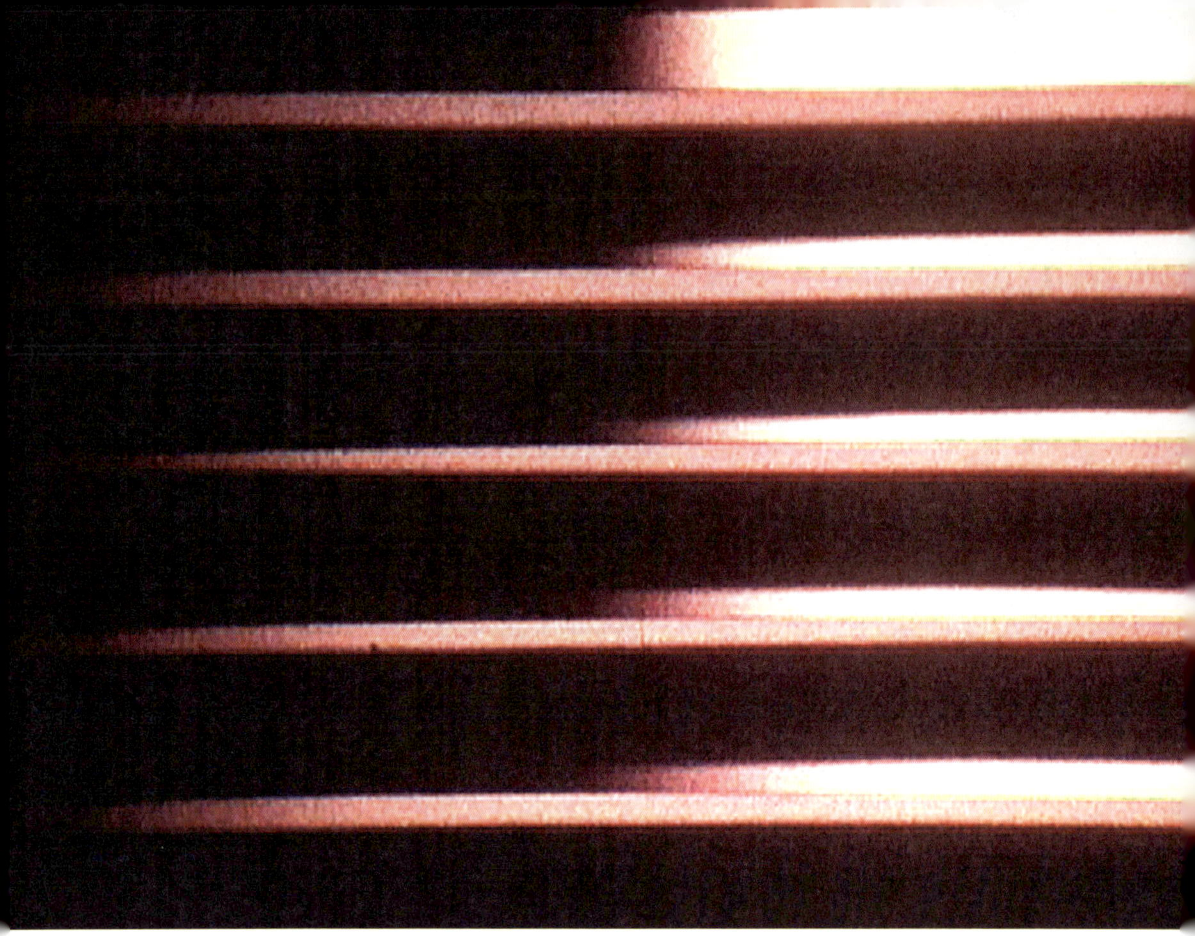

Horizontal, 1979
Still from 3.37 min single-channel video

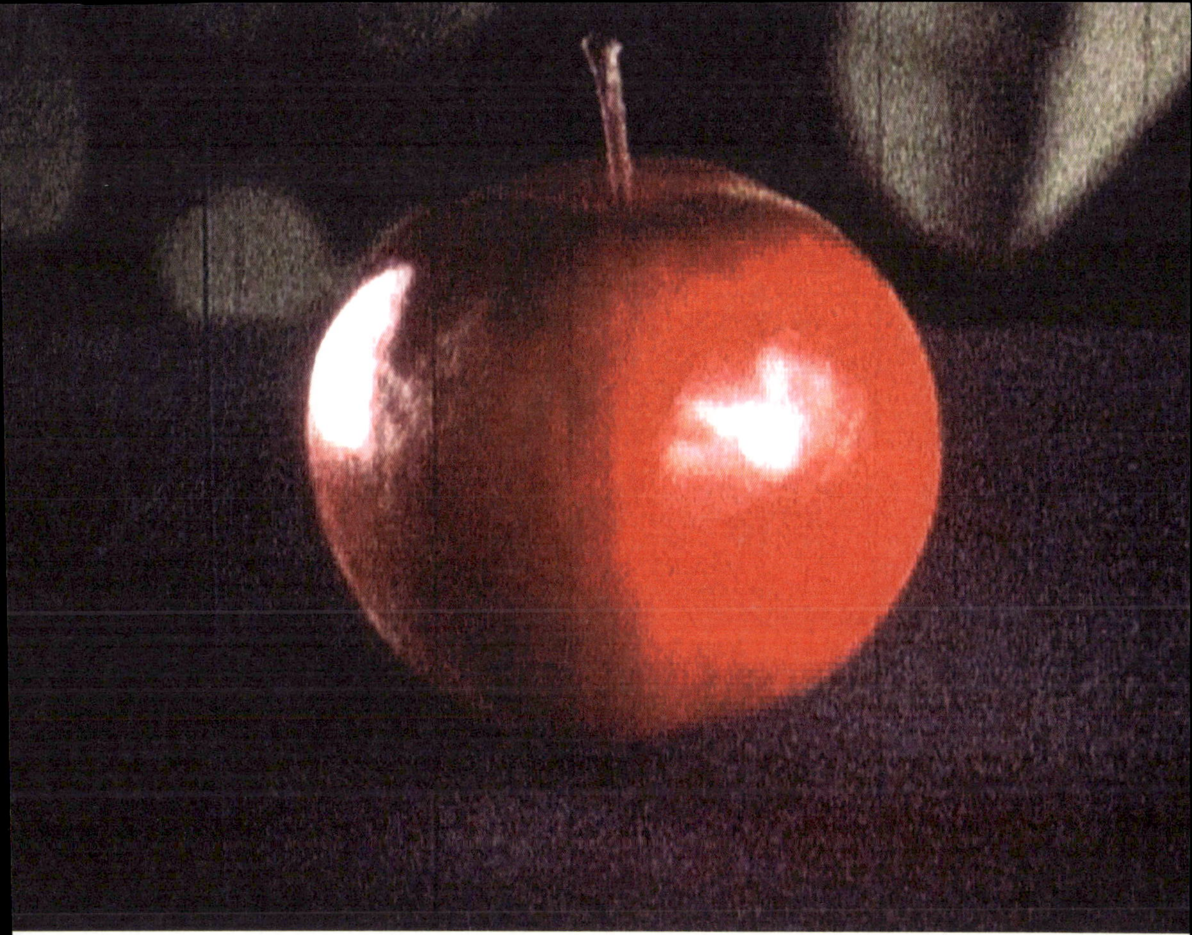

The Apple, 1976
Still from 1.05 min 16mm film, color,
optical sound, transferred from Super-8

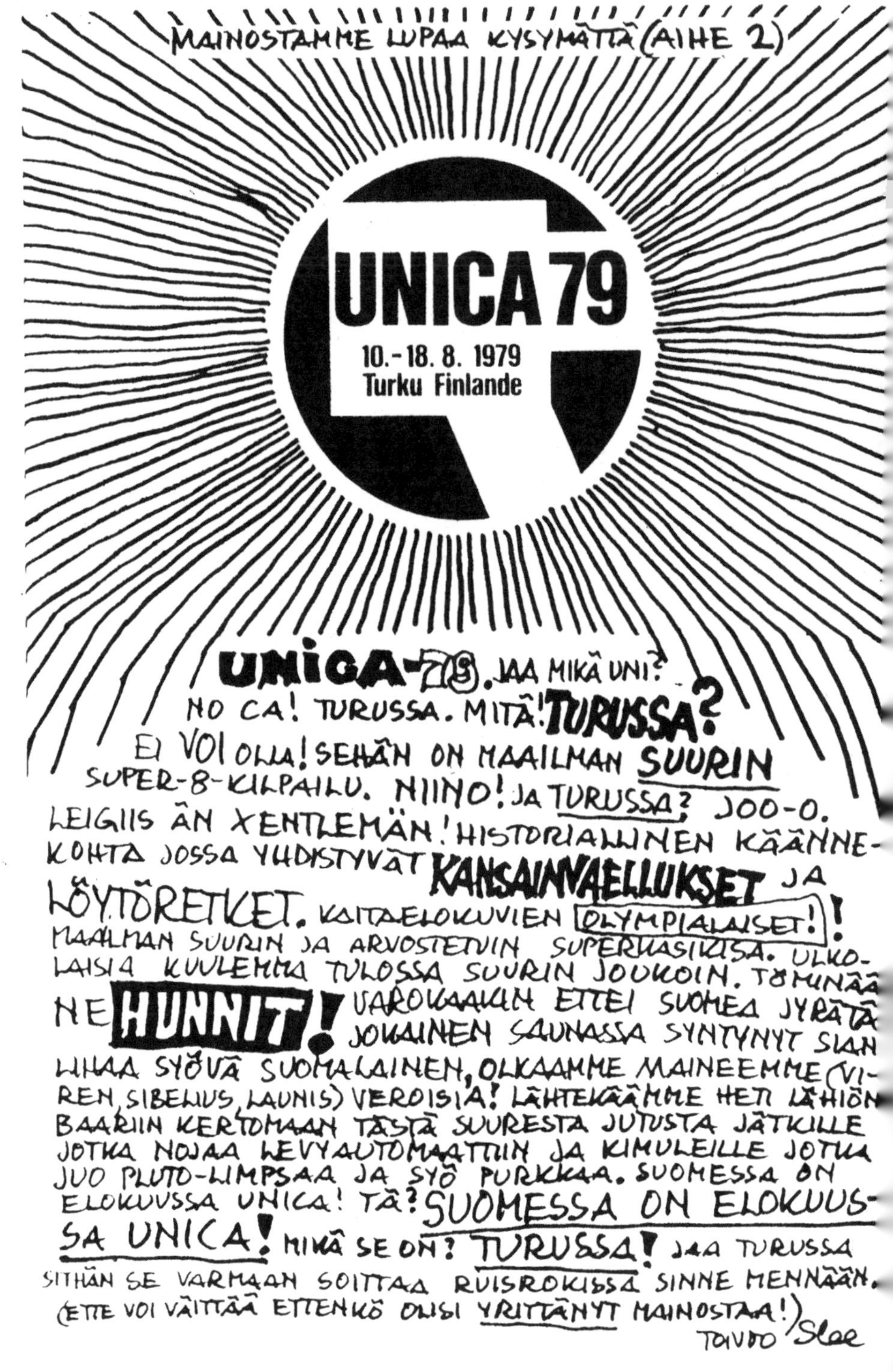
MAINOSTAMME LUPAA KYSYMÄTTÄ (AIHE 2)

UNICA 79
10.–18. 8. 1979
Turku Finlande

UNIGA-79. JAA MIKÄ UNI? NO CA! TURUSSA. MITÄ! TURUSSA? EI VOI OLLA! SEHÄN ON MAAILMAN SUURIN SUPER-8-KILPAILU. NIINO! JA TURUSSA? JOO-O. LEIGIIS ÄN XENTREMÄN! HISTORIALLINEN KÄÄNNEKOHTA JOSSA YHDISTYVÄT KANSAINVAELLUKSET JA LÖYTÖRETKET. KAITAELOKUVIEN OLYMPIALAISET!! MAAILMAN SUURIN JA ARVOSTETUIN SUPERKASIKISA. ULKOLAISIA KUULEMMA TULOSSA SUURIN JOUKOIN. TOMINÄÄ NE HUNNIT! VAROKAAKIN ETTEI SUOMEA JYRÄTÄ. JOKAINEN SAUNASSA SYNTYNYT SIANLIHAA SYÖVÄ SUOMALAINEN, OLKAAMME MAINEEMME (VIREN, SIBELIUS, LAUNIS) VEROISIA! LÄHTEKÄÄMME HETI LÄHIÖN BAARIIN KERTOMAAN TÄSTÄ SUURESTA JUTUSTA JÄTKILLE JOTKA NOJAA LEVYAUTOMAATTIIN JA KIMULEILLE JOTKA JUO PLUTO-LIMPSAA JA SYÖ PURKKAA. SUOMESSA ON ELOKUUSSA UNICA! TÄ? SUOMESSA ON ELOKUUSSA UNICA! MIKÄ SE ON? TURUSSA! JAA TURUSSA SITHÄN SE VARMAAN SOITTAA RUISROKISSA SINNE MENNÄÄN. (ETTE VOI VÄITTÄÄ ETTENKÖ OLISI YRITTÄNYT MAINOSTAA!)

TOIVO Slee

Spread from *Underground Super 8 Film* fanzine, issue 2, 1979

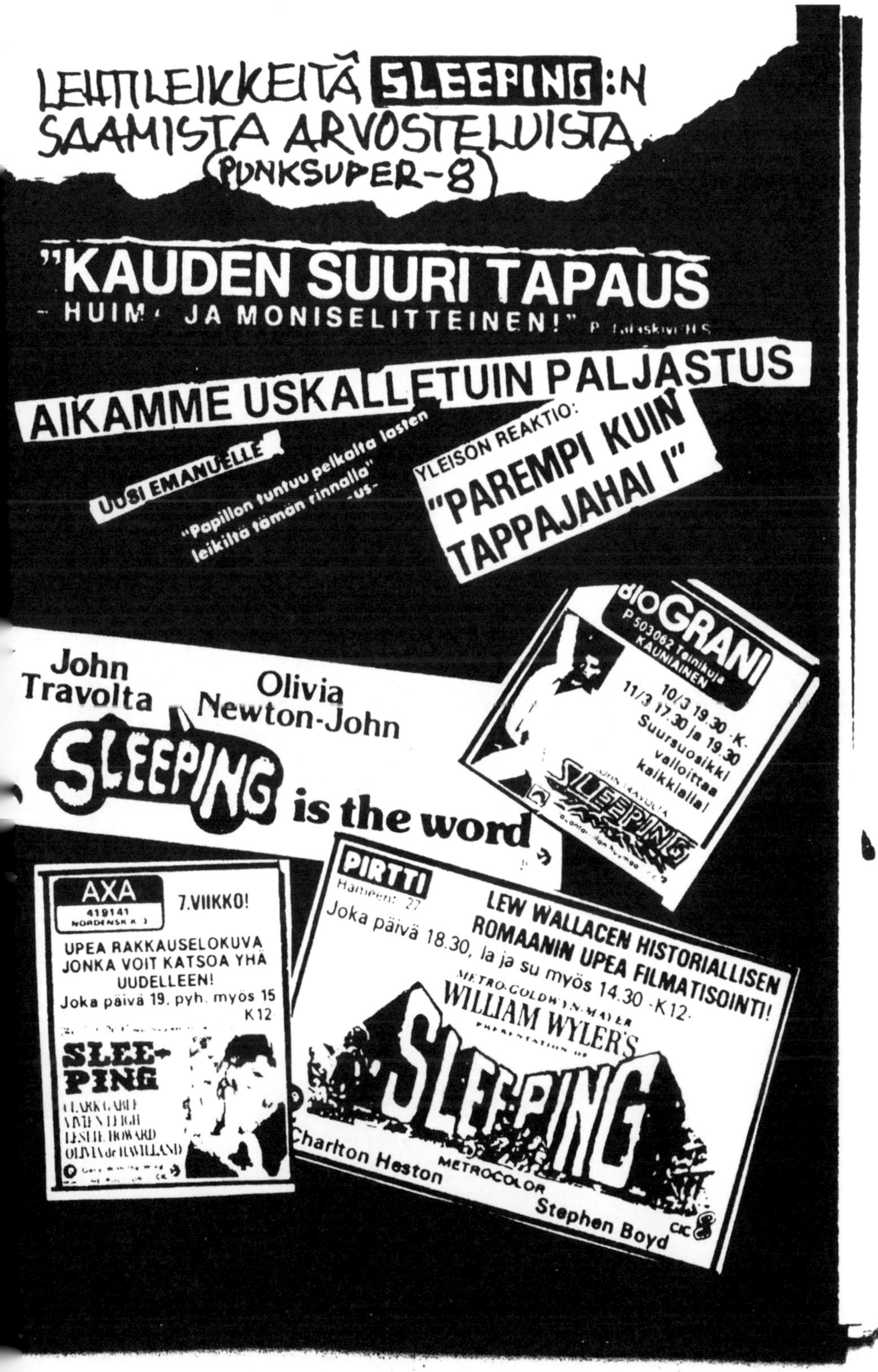
LEHTILEIKKEITÄ SLEEPING:N
SAAMISTA ARVOSTELUISTA
(PUNKSUPER-8)
"KAUDEN SUURI TAPAUS
JA MONISELITTEINEN!"
AIKAMME USKALLETUIN PALJASTUS
UUSI EMANUELLE
"Papillon tuntuu pelkalta lasten leikiltä tämän rinnalla"
-us-
YLEISÖN REAKTIO:
"PAREMPI KUIN TAPPAJAHAI I"
BioGRANI
KAUNIAINEN
10/3 19.30 -K-
11/3 17.30 ja 19.30
Suursuosikki valloittaa kaikkialla!
SLEEPING
John Travolta
Olivia Newton-John
SLEEPING is the word
AXA
419141
7.VIIKKO!
UPEA RAKKAUSELOKUVA JONKA VOIT KATSOA YHÄ UUDELLEEN!
Joka päivä 19, pyh. myös 15
K12
SLEE-PING
CLARK GABLE
VIVIEN LEIGH
LESLIE HOWARD
OLIVIA de HAVILLAND
PIRTTI
Joka päivä 18.30, la ja su myös 14.30 -K12-
LEW WALLACEN HISTORIALLISEN ROMAANIN UPEA FILMATISOINTI!
METRO-GOLDWYN-MAYER
WILLIAM WYLER'S
SLEEPING
Charlton Heston
METROCOLOR
Stephen Boyd
CIC

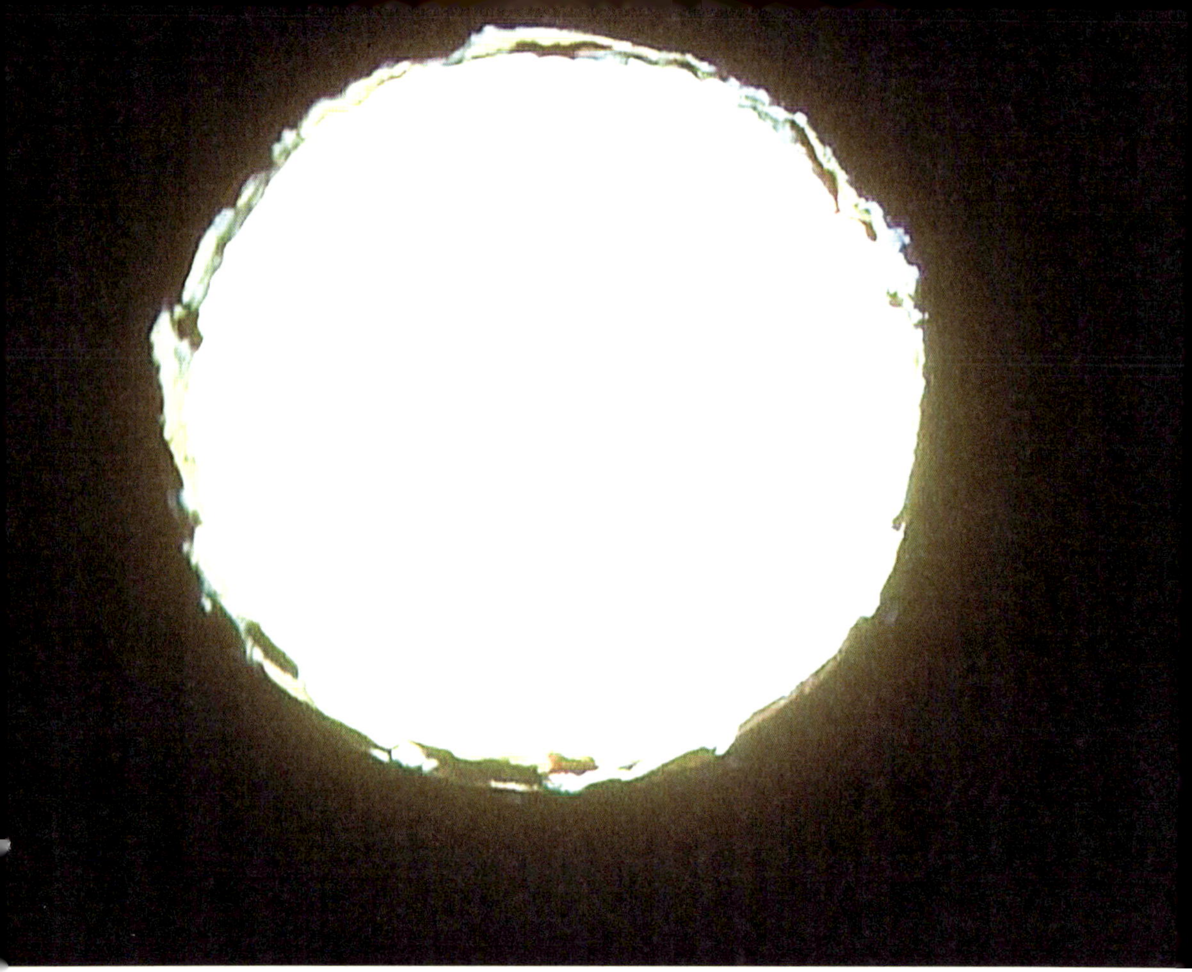

Five Holes in Celluloid, 1980
Still from 16mm film, color, optical sound,
transferred from Super-8

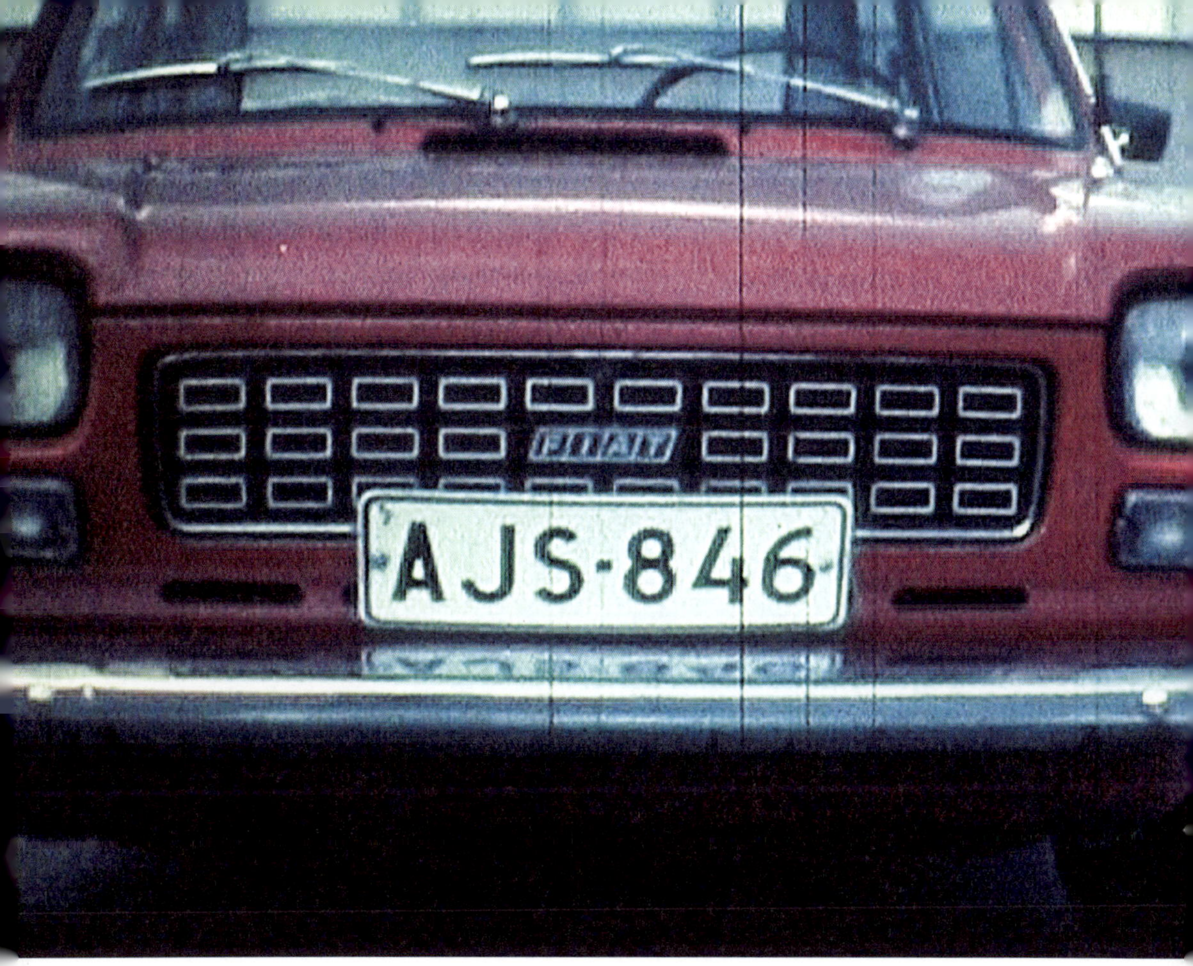

3000 Cars, 1980
Still from 16mm film, color, optical sound,
transferred from Super-8

“Fill the Screen with Stuff”: The Energy and Expressiveness of Pasi “Sleeping” Myllymäki’s Short Films

by Tytti Rantanen

If Georges Méliès (1861–1938) were reborn as a punk rocker in postwar Finland, his filmic output might come close to Pasi “Sleeping” Myllymäki’s (b. 1950) uninhibited DIY films. At the same time, this comparison is imprecise, because whereas Méliès is enthroned as the pioneer of fiction film, Myllymäki mostly aims beyond the frame of fiction—or even narrative. According to Myllymäki, the distinctiveness of experimental film is that it happens to the viewer instead of to a fictive protagonist that the viewer can observe from a safe distance.[1] What further connects Myllymäki to Méliès and another pioneer of moving images, Robert W. Paul (1869–1943), is an essential fascination with visual tricks and gimmicks, and the joy of experimenting with the cinematic medium.

After graduating as a graphic designer from the Lahti Institute of Crafts and Design in 1976, Myllymäki worked in the visual design department at the Iittala glassworks. A passionate lover of cinema, the visual arts, literature, and punk rock, he found a partner in crime in Risto “Legend” Laakkonen, with whom he shot nearly fifty Super-8 underground films between 1976 and 1985, the first one being

The Apple. As an extension of filmmaking and a forum for his frustration with the conservative Super 8 society in Finland, Myllymäki also published a zine called *Maanalainen kaitaelokuva* (Underground Super 8 Film).

Myllymäki's background as a graphic designer is apparent in how much weight he gives to the opening and (especially) the end credits. They can be stylized as such, but occasionally the expressive content of the film is stretched onto them, as in *To Be Continued* (1982), where the whole drama of the film evolves from the repeated cancellation of the end credits. In another work, the Finnish word for "The End" (*LOPPU*) is reworked into the nonsensical word *EORBA*, hence the title of the work (1980). Yet despite being bursts of punk-rock spirit, Myllymäki's films are *also* finished pieces of artisanal moving imagery. Most of his films have a DIY soundtrack with effects and noise made with an electric guitar or a shortwave radio receiver. Myllymäki designs the relationship between sound and image carefully, yet creatively.

Myllymäki's cinematic poetics do not follow any rules. He is led by intuition, curiosity, and expressive freedom. His philosophy and practice are that any finished film is better than all of those that were never even shot.

The films are minimalist in setting and visual content (like the cameraless *Five Holes in Celluloid* [1980]), but rich in their imaginative means. Many are nonfigurative, but not all. *The Forssa Syndrome* (1982) is a hilarious mockumentary about a small town where people walk, run, and even cycle backward. The themes range from concerns over the nuclear threat in the 1980s to sexuality and social criticism.

There are several layers of influence and inspiration in Myllymäki's films. If different tricks such as reverse or stop motion evoke an association with early cinema, piercing and scratching the celluloid attach him to the modernist avant-garde tradition—for instance Stan Brakhage (1933–2003), Norman McLaren (1914–1987), or the Finnish "cinematic action painter" Eino Ruutsalo (1921–2001). Myllymäki has reportedly been inspired by at least the latter two.[2] *An Andalusian Doghouse* (1980) obviously pays homage to Luis Buñuel (1900–1983) and Salvador Dalí (1904–1989), while *Un Chien Andalou*'s (1929) iconic shot of an eye being cut is alluded to in Myllymäki's film manifesto *Sleeping* (1979), which is also the source of his stage name.

With *Sleeping*, Myllymäki aspired to shake the Finnish Super 8 society awake from its apathy.[3] The schism between underground and established Super 8 circles is a recurring topic of Myllymäki's films to the extent that it sounds comic to someone born after 1980. However, the quarrel is worth contextualizing. The Finnish Federation for Amateur Film-makers has tried to censor Myllymäki in different competitions, as his expressive audacity was something that had not been seen since the underground films of the late 1960s and early 1970s. Video art had not yet made a breakthrough in Finland in the early 1980s. At the time, there were only two television channels. The avant-garde was blossoming more among small theater groups than within moving image. No more than ten years earlier, the Finnish underground artist Mattijuhani Koponen had been incarcerated for simulating sexual intercourse in a performance.

Myllymäki's films have screened at international UNICA festivals, also known as "the Super 8 Olympics." Despite being dismissed by conservative amateur filmmakers, Myllymäki had friends and supporters among art students and other avant-garde artists. Even if the domestic establishment was slow to warm up to them, the works were appreciated on a Scandinavian scale to the extent that the Swedish filmmaker and curator of the Moderna Museet in Stockholm, Claes Söderquist, purchased ten films in 16mm format for the museum's collection as early as 1982.[4]

There has been an ongoing renaissance of Pasi "Sleeping" Myllymäki's art since the extensive retrospective curated by Mika Taanila for the Avanto Festival in 2006. His films have been screened at various international events over the past ten years. Myllymäki has confessed on several occasions to preferring the company of punk rockers to that of culture snobs.
I spent most of the Mänttä Art Festival 2016 opening ceremony in a dark room watching his retrospective, and witnessed two elderly ladies provoked at the deliberate repetitiveness of one of the films (*The Tape Recorder Is a Wonderful Invention* [1983]). I reported this to the artist: his works still get under the skin of the petit bourgeoisie! He grinned and seemed pleased.

Notes

1 Mika Taanila, "Seitsemännen taiteen sivullisia. Kokeellinen elokuva Suomessa 1933–1985." [Outsiders of the Seventh Art: Finnish Experimental Cinema 1933–1985], in *Sähkömetsä. Suomalaisen videotaiteen ja kokeellisen elokuvan historiaa 1933–1998*, ed. Kirsi Väkiparta (Helsinki: Valtion taidemuseo / Kuvataiteen keskusarkisto, 2007, 10–41); Pasi Myllymäki, artist talk at Malmitalo, March 5, 2010, http://puoltaja.fi/yleinen/kauniita-uneksijoita-malmilla.

2 Mika Taanila, "Seitsemännen taiteen sivullisia"; Pasi Myllymäki, artist talk at Mänttä Art Festival, August 6, 2016, http://kuvataideviikot.fi/doc/yleista_2016/luento06082016_mita_sleeping_todella_sanoi.pdf.

3 *Maanalainen kaitaelokuva nro 1*, 16.3.1979, Iittala, http://oranssi.net/pienlehdet/lehdet/output-166.pdf; Mika Taanila, "Outsiders of the Seventh Art"; Pasi Myllymäki, artist talk at Mänttä Art Festival, August 6, 2016.

4 Mika Taanila, "Seitsemännen taiteen sivullisia."

Mika Taanila

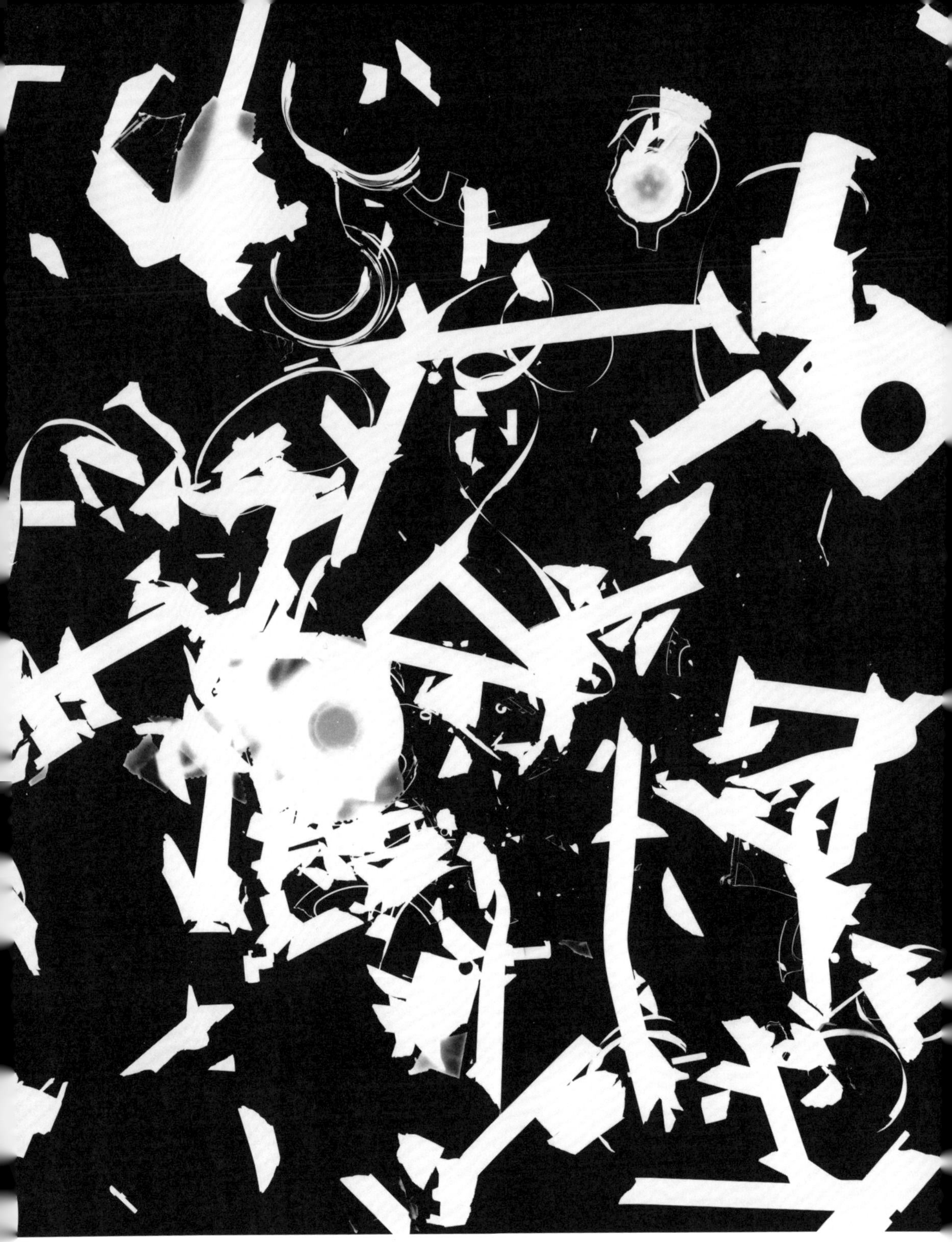

Strait-Jacket, from the series
Black and White Movies, 2013
Pigment print
60 × 72 cm, framed 75 × 87 cm

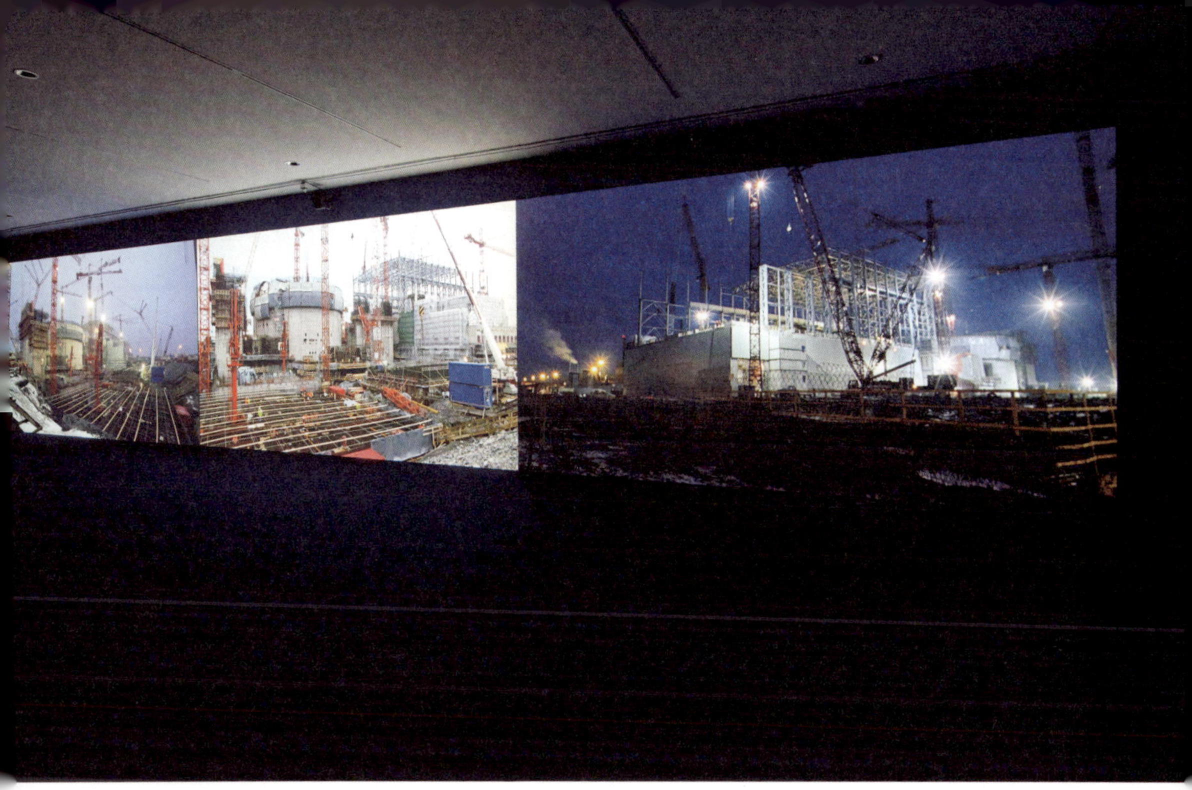

The Most Electrified Town in Finland, 2012
Three-channel video installation, digital files, 15 min, color, 300 x 1600 cm
Installation view, dOCUMENTA (13), Kassel

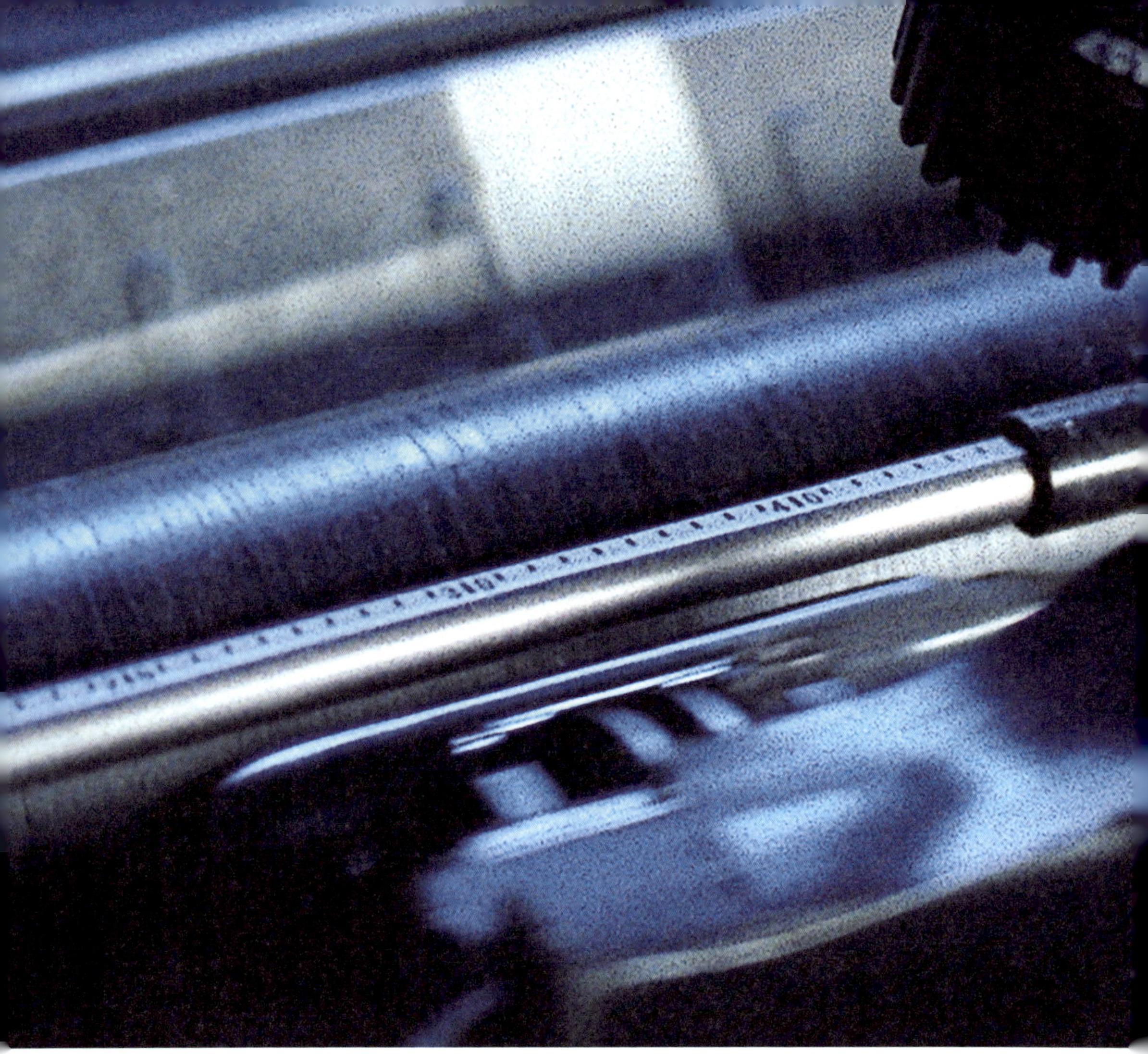

Optical Sound, 2005
Short film, 35mm, 6 min, color and b/w

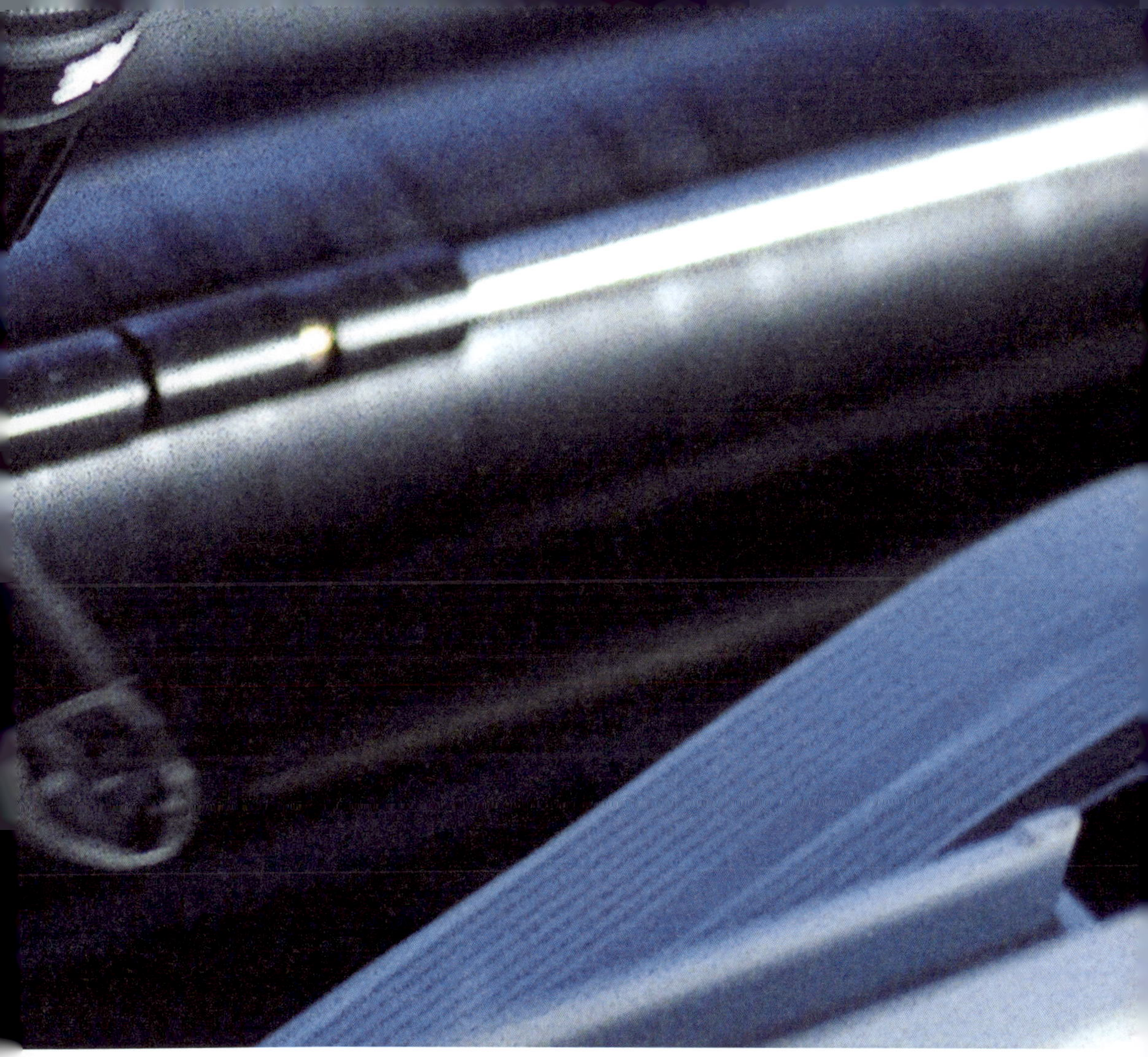

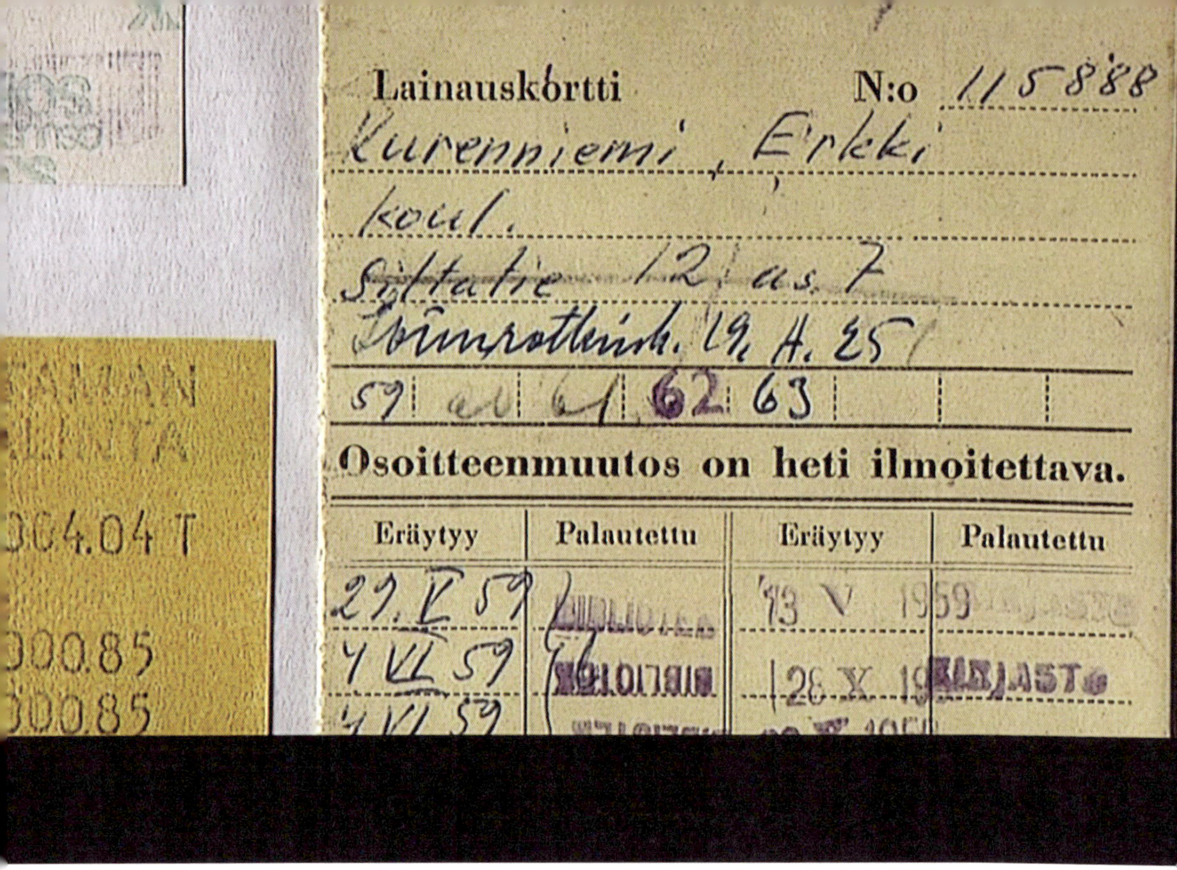

Future Is Not What It Used to Be, 2002
Documentary film, 35mm, 52 min, color and b/w

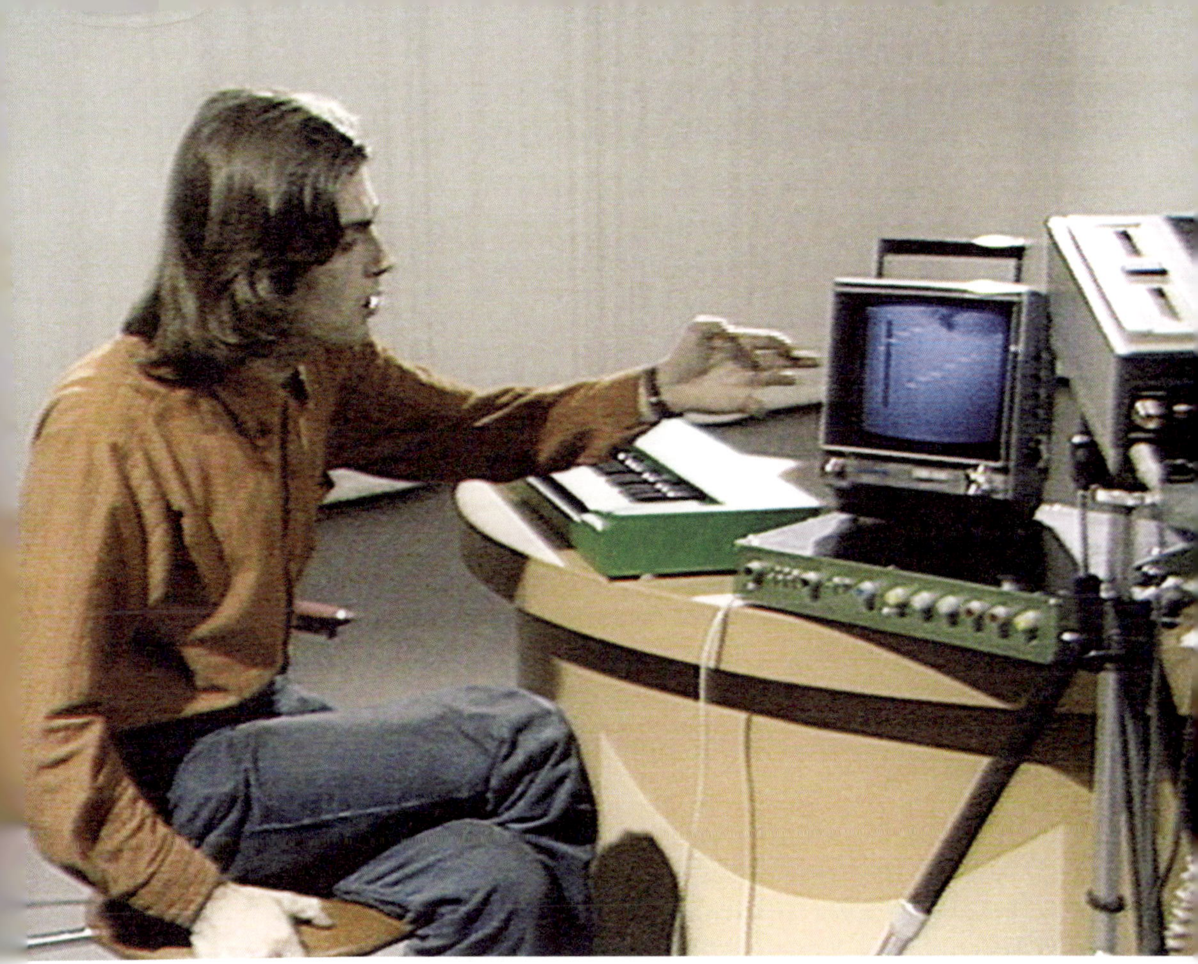

Future Is Not What It Used To Be, 2002
Documentary film, 35mm, 52 min, color and b/w

Reverse Engineering
by Edwin Carels

What if the first person to live five hundred years has already been born? How will he or she remain occupied, as prognoses state that in a mere twenty years, automation will replace two thirds of all employment? And what if the Google Brain research experiment indeed runs out of control and computers start to use a language of their own invention, indecipherable to human intelligence? These are just a few of the many tantalizing scenarios for the future currently propagated by the media.

With telling titles such as *Futuro—A New Stance for Tomorrow* (1998) and *Future Is Not What It Used to Be* (2002), Mika Taanila (b. 1965) investigates speculations about the future. Yet the artist is far from a futurologist. As his visual essays illustrate, he is more interested in case studies from the past, peculiar practices that by now are largely forgotten. *Thank You for the Music* (1997) for instance reminds us of the Muzak corporation, a company that for many decades controlled the airwaves of shopping malls all over the Western world. More than simply a portrayal of silly hobbyists, *RoboCup99* (2000), made on the brink of the new millennium, signals the first steps of robots that transgress from the workplace into the leisure space.

As is clear from his steady and surprisingly diverse output (films, installations, photography, music, objects) Taanila systematically raises questions about the techno-driven imagination of humankind. Who came up with the idea of composing music that is meant to go unnoticed? What drives certain individuals to organize soccer tournaments for self-made robots? Who wants to market orange plastic inhabitable eggs? Why revive the nineteenth-century practice of pedestrianism (*Six Day Run* [2013])? With the eye of an anthropologist (his initial choice in higher education) Taanila investigates the "otherworldliness of this world" by portraying idiosyncratic people and singular events. His body of work appears like a catalog of forgotten experiments, sometimes quite literally resurrecting discarded films of scientific tests, as with the installations *A Physical Ring* (2002), *The Zone of Total Eclipse* (2006), and *Twilight* (2010).

Although Taanila clearly revels in the materiality of outdated technology (such as the noise of dot-matrix printers, in *Optical Sound* [2005]), his interests are not those of a regressive sentimentalist or a retro-futurist. Having obtained his artist's diploma in crafts and design at Lahti's Institute of Design and Fine Arts in 1992, Taanila never simply focuses on anachronistic aesthetics, but rather on how society designs and defines itself through the use of technology. A study of distortion on VHS tapes (*Verbranntes Land* [2002]) also functions as a reminder that all media distort while storing information. His works are not intended as "time machines" that aim to propel us back; they are investigations of the "machine times" that we live in. Chronicling the construction of the world's most powerful nuclear power plant, the documentary *Return of the Atom* (2015, co-directed with Jussi Eerola) clearly demonstrates how contemporary Taanila's concerns are.

An earlier version of this project, the triple-screen installation *The Most Electrified Town in Finland* (2012), premiered at dOCUMENTA (13). Concurrently, a large section of the same exhibition venue was devoted to Erkki Kurenniemi, Finland's forgotten pioneer of electronic music as well as a visionary designer, philosopher, and artist, who was already speculating about artificial intelligence in the 1960s. It was Taanila who revived popular interest in Kurenniemi with his film *Future Is Not What It Used to Be*, and the expanded DVD release *The Dawn of Dimi* (2002).

One of the underlying themes of dOCUMENTA (13) was media archaeology, a questioning of progress by looking back at past technologies. Informed by Foucauldian concepts, media archaeologists respond to the naive neophilia surrounding the digital revolution. Starting in the mid-1990s, with Bruce Sterling launching his *Dead Media Manifesto*, media archeology opened up both in theory and in practice alternative perspectives to media history, "to find the old in the new and new in the old."[1] Tellingly, one of media archaeology's prominent voices, Erkki Huhtamo, was Taanila's conversation partner from very early on.

Besides anthropology and media archaeology, two more frameworks provide extra coherence to Taanila's complex oeuvre: music and curatorship. These can also help explain the radicality of recent "destructivist," "anarchaeologist" works such as *Black and White Movies* (2013). In 1980, while still living with his parents, Taanila's first output was a series of lo-fi tape recordings on cassettes (rereleased on CD in 2009 as *Musiikkivyöry: Tulemme sokeiksi*). Inspired by the punk movement, and more specifically the first wave of industrial music, Taanila started out by creating and distributing music. Initiating the cassette label Valtavat ihmesilmälasit together with Anton Nikkilä was his first curatorial effort, and his first film release was *The Double* (1993), a VHS compilation of Russian industrial music and low-tech videos, also a collaboration with Nikkilä. Soon after, Taanila began to shoot music videos for friends' bands, parallel to developing his own oeuvre.[2]

This supportive role may indicate why Taanila has always avoided a typical narrator's voice in documentary projects. Another explanation is the postmodern claim of the end of history, or at least the end of grand narratives. The background against which Taanila started exhibiting internationally was the collapse of the Soviet Union and the fall of the Iron Curtain, which lay the field open for globalization, worldwide digitization, and rampant neoliberalism. Around the time of his first participation in an exhibition (*The Day of the Donkey Day*, Transmission Gallery, Glasgow, 1999), Taanila also lay the foundations of the Avanto Festival, an annual event of nonconformist music and moving images in his hometown of Helsinki.

From 2000 until 2008 he remained one of the most consistent programmers there, showcasing his passions in music and film, as well as providing further context for his own creative output. Avanto's 2002 opening night offered for instance an homage to Kurenniemi, complementing the premiere of his film with a reconstruction of an early interactive dance performance and a live performance by the band Pan Sonic using original instruments by Kurenniemi. With each edition Avanto significantly combined the most adventurous electronic music with the living legacy of structuralist filmmaking from the 1970s.

This culminated in the final years of the festival with the attendance of avant-garde legends Tony Conrad, Michael Snow (who both had careers in music as well as film), Peter Kubelka, Ken Jacobs, and a special focus on Guy Debord. Just as Taanila's curatorial contribution to the 2014 Oberhausen festival, *Memories Can't Wait: Film without Film*, can be understood as a thinking exercise to develop his own cameraless film *Tectonic Plate* (2016), his programs for Avanto are strongly indicative of his own creative criteria. From the tradition of structuralist film and paracinema in the 1970s, Taanila adopted a critical, deconstructive attitude toward audiovisual *dispositifs*.

Against this background, his most recent work with destroyed movie books gains much more significance than merely a punk statement, or a nod toward John Latham's strategy of destroying art history books. From shooting on film to shooting film books, as a postindustrial Proust, Taanila counters the techno-materialist underpinnings of an economy under the sign of creative destruction and cultivated obsolescence. A psycho-geographer of these machine times, he holds up a mirror to the deceptive ephemerality of the digital. Because no car is safe without rearview mirrors.

Notes

1 For a contextualization of media archaeology's genealogy, see for instance Wanda Strauven, "Media Archaeology: Where Film History, Media Art, and New Media (Can) Meet," in *Preserving and Exhibiting Media Art*, ed. Julia Noordergraaf, Cosetta G. Saba, Barbara Le Maître, and Vinzen Hediger (Amsterdam: Amsterdam University Press, 2013), 59–79.

2 For more details on these early music videos, see Olaf Möller, "Time Indefinite According to the Laws of Thermodynamics," in *Mika Taanila—Aikakoneita / Time Machines*, ed. Leevi Haapala and Kati T. Kivinen (Helsinki: Kiasma, 2013), 26.

Siri Aurdal (b. 1937) lives and works in Oslo, Norway. Aurdal has exhibited at Oslo Kunstforening; Kunstnernes Hus, Oslo; and Murray Guy, New York. Ausal has participated in group exhibitions at Arkiv för dekorativ konst / Skissernas Museum, Lund; the 15th Biennial, Antwerp; Kunsthall Oslo; and Stavanger Kunsthall. A major sculptural work, *Wavelengths Recomposed*, was installed in Oslo's Vigelandparken in 2016, as a joint project between Kunstnernes Hus and OSLO PILOT, Kulturetaten, the City of Oslo.

Nina Canell (b. 1979) lives and works in Berlin, Germany. Canell has exhibited at Kunsthalle Fridericianum, Kassel; Hamburger Bahnhof, Berlin; Camden Arts Centre, London; Douglas Hyde Gallery, Dublin; Moderna Museet, Stockholm; Arko Art Center, Seoul; and in 2017 at Museum Tamayo, Mexico City. She has participated in various group exhibitions at important art institutions, including Biennale de Lyon; Sydney Biennale; Palais de Tokyo, Paris; Museum of Modern Art, New York; Liverpool Biennale; Tate Liverpool; and Manifesta 7, Rovereto. Canell was an Edstrandska Stiftelsen laureate in 2011, and was awarded the ars viva Prize for Visual Arts the same year. canellwatkins.org

Charlotte Johannesson (b. 1943) lives and works in Skanör, Sweden. She has exhibited at Galerie S:t Petri, Lund, Konstmuseet, Ystad, Galleri Glemminge, Gelmmingebro, Galerie Green, Malmö, Dexter Bang Sinister, Charlottenborg, Copenhagen, and Galleri Petra Lilja, Malmö, and has participated in various group exhibitions, including the 32nd São Paolo Biennial, the Van Abbemuseum, Eindhoven, Barbican Art Gallery, London, Göteborgs Konstmuseum, Norrköpings Konstmuseum, Museum of Modern Art, Toyama, Pratt Center, New York, Academy of Art College Gallery, San Francisco; Musée d'Art Moderne de la Ville de Paris; Air Gallery, New York; Malmö Konsthall; and Kulturhuset, Stockholm. Johannesson was awarded the Royal Swedish Academy of Arts scholarship in 1976. In 2016, she was a laureate of the Aase & Richard Björklund Fund.

Jumana Manna (b. 1987) lives and works in Berlin, Germany. She has exhibited at Sculpture Center, New York; Chisenhale Gallery, London, Kunsthall Oslo; and Beirut Art Center.
She has participated in group exhibitions at Kunsthalle Wien; Liverpool Biennial; Marrakech Biennale 6; the Jerusalem Show VII; Al Ma'mal Foundation; Museum of Modern Arts Warsaw; and Henie Onstad Kunstsenter, Bærum.
Manna's films have been screened at festivals including Berlinale Forum; BAFICI; FID Marseille; Viennale; New Horizons

Wroclaw; and International Film Festival, Rotterdam. She was awarded the A.M. Qattan Foundation's Young Palestinian Artist Award in 2012 and is the ars viva Prize for Visual Arts laureate in 2017. jumanamanna.com

Pasi "Sleeping" Myllymäki (b. 1950) is a filmmaker based in Hämeenlinna, Finland. Myllymäki's films have been screened widely at festivals and art institutions in Finland and internationally, including Unica, Baku; The Kitchen, New York; Hämeenlinna Art Museum; Moderna Museet, Stockholm; Rajaton Elokuva Event, Joensuu; Avanto Festival, Kiasma, Helsinki; Nordisk Panorama, Oulu; VIDEO-EX, Zürich; Kauniita uneksijoita-event; Kino Kaiku, Malmitalo, Helsinki; Avant Goes Witty, Karlstad; International Film Festival, Rotterdam; Kinos Festival, Lahti; AAVE Festival, Helsinki; Rakkautta ja Anarkiaa Film Festival, Helsinki; and VIDEOMEDEJA Film Festival Novi Sad.

Mika Taanila (b. 1965) lives and works in Helsinki, Finland. He has exhibited at Kiasma Museum of Contemporary Art in Helsinki, Contemporary Art Museum St. Louis, Migrosmuseum, Zürich, and Badischer Kunstverein, Karlsruhe. He has participated in the group exhibitions dOCUMENTA (13), Kassel; Aichi Triennale, Nagoya; Manifesta 4, Frankfurt-am-Main; and Shanghai Biennale. Taanila's films have been screened at numerous international film festivals and special events, including the Toronto International Film Festival; International Film Festival, Rotterdam; Berlinale; CPH:DOX; International Short Film Festival, Clermont-Ferrand; Midnight Sun Film Festival, Sodankylä; and Oberhausen Kurzfilmtage. In 2015, he was presented with the Ars Fennica Award. mikataanila.com

Kirsty Bell is a writer and critic living in Berlin. A contributing editor to *frieze* magazine, she also writes for *Art in America*, *Art Agenda*, *Mousse*, *Parkett*, and *Camera Austria*, and had published numerous monographic catalogue essays. Her book *The Artist's House: From Workplace to Artwork* was published by Sternberg Press in 2013.

Edwin Carels is a teacher and researcher at the School of Arts KASK/HoGent. He holds a PhD in the arts, and is currently working on a postdoctoral project under the title *Counter-archives*. Carels is also active as a film programmer and curator for the International Film Festival Rotterdam, and as a writer he publishes essays on media archaeology, visual arts, film, and animation.

Tytti Rantanen is a program coordinator at AV-arkki, the distribution center for Finnish media art. She is also editor in chief of *niin & näin*, a Finnish philosophical magazine. She is currently finishing her PhD on narrative sabotage in French experimental literature and film of the 1960s and 1970s.

Chris Sharp is a writer and independent curator based in Mexico City. He is the cofounder of the Mexico City independent space Lulu and a contributing editor at *Art Review* and *Art Agenda*, and his writing has appeared in many magazines, online publications, and catalogues.

Mats Stjernstedt is director of Malmö Konsthall since January 2017. From 2011 to 2016 he was director of Kunstnernes Hus in Oslo, and from 2001 to 2009 he was the head of Index – the Swedish Contemporary Art Foundation, Stockholm. Stjernstedt has curated numerous international exhibitions and projects since the mid-1990s. He has also been an art critic for *Aftonbladet*, *Artforum*, *Flash Art*, and *Art + Text*.

Cecilia Widenheim has been director of Malmö Konstmuseum since 2012. Between 2008 and 2010 she was director of Iaspis, the international program for visual arts, design, and architecture of the Swedish Arts Grants Committee. For many years she was a curator at the Moderna Museet in Stockholm, responsible for the collection of Swedish and Nordic modern and contemporary art. Widenheim is also active as a lecturer, writer, and editor.

Kaelen Wilson-Goldie is a journalist and critic and a contributing editor for *Bidoun*. She writes regularly for *Artforum*, *Bookforum*, *Aperture*, and *frieze*, and teaches in the Department of Fine Arts and Art History at the American University of Beirut, and in the School of Visual Arts at the Académie Libanaise des Beaux-Arts.

Photographic credits

Siri Aurdal

16	Eline Mugaas
17	Morten Krogh
18	Eline Mugaas

Nina Canell

28	Mother's Tankstation / Leo Xu Projects
29–30	Nick Ash
30	Nick Ash
31	Robin Watkins
32	Andy Keate

Charlotte Johannesson

40–47	Albin Dahlström / Moderna Museet

Jumana Manna

58	Thorvaldsen / Henie Onstad Kunstsenter
59	David Smith / Courtesy the artist and CRG Gallery, New York
62	Marco Pinarelli / Beirut Art Center / Courtesy the artist and CRG Gallery, New York

Mika Taanila

86	Courtesy the artist and balzer projects
87	Anders Sune Berg / dOCUMENTA (13) / Courtesy the artist and Kinotar Oy
88	Jussi Eerola / Kinotar Oy
90–91	Kinotar Oy

The catalogue is published in conjunction with the exhibition *Mirrored* at the Nordic Pavilion, 57th International Art Exhibition, Biennale di Venezia, Venice

Commissioners:
Ann-Sofi Noring, Moderna Museet (Sweden) with Katya García-Antón, Office for Contemporary Art Norway, OCA (Norway) and Raija Koli, Frame Contemporary Art (Finland)

Exhibition:
Curator: Mats Stjernstedt
Project manager: Matilda Olof-Ors

Acknowledgements:
Allegrini
Arts Promotion Center Finland – National Council for the Visual Arts
Barbro Osher Pro Suecia Foundation
Nordic Circle for Venice

THE BARBRO OSHER PRO SUECIA FOUNDATION

Allegrini

Catalogue

Editor: Mats Stjernstedt
Managing editors: Stefano Cernuschi,
Teresa Hahr
Copy editor: Lindsey Westbrook
Picture editor: Guy Engström
Translation: Gabriella Berggren,
Jan Salomonsson, Saskia Vogel
Graphic design: Mousse
Printed and bound in Italy by Artigiana Grafica

Co-published by Moderna Museet and
Mousse Publishing

ISBN 978-91-863243-88-3 (Moderna Museet)
ISBN 978-88-6749-273-2 (Mousse Publishing)

www.modernamuseet.se
www.moussepublishing.com